spring-summer 2025

Mission

The *Community Literacy Journal* is is an interdisciplinary journal that publishes both scholarly work that contributes to theories, methodologies, and research agendas and work by literacy workers, practitioners, and community literacy program staff. We are especially committed to presenting work done in collaboration between academics and community members, organizers, activists, teachers, and artists.

We understand "community literacy" as including multiple domains for literacy work extending beyond mainstream educational and work institutions. It can be found in programs devoted to adult education, early childhood education, reading initiatives, or work with marginalized populations. It can also be found in more informal, ad hoc projects, including creative writing, graffiti art, protest songwriting, and social media campaigns.

For us, literacy is defined as the realm where attention is paid not just to content or to knowledge but to the symbolic means by which it is represented and used. Thus, literacy refers not just to letters and to text but to other multimodal, technological, and embodied representations, as well. Community literacy is interdisciplinary and intersectional in nature, drawing from rhetoric and composition, communication, literacy studies, English studies, gender studies, race and ethnic studies, environmental studies, critical theory, linguistics, cultural studies, education, and more.

Cover Artist and Art

"Sound Station from Bautista and Jeannin's 'Collective Walk on How We Read and Listen to the Environment, History, and Each Other.'" World Congress of Environmental History, Oulu (FI), August 2024. Image credit: L. Catchings.

Submissions

Submissions for the Articles section of the journal should clearly demonstrate engagement with community literacy scholarship, particularly scholarship previously published in the *Community Literacy Journal*. The editors seek work that pushes the field forward in exciting and perhaps unexpected ways. Case studies, qualitative and/or quantitative research, conceptual articles, etc., ranging from 25-30 manuscript pages, are welcome. If deemed appropriate, we will send the manuscript out to readers for blind review. You can expect a report in approximately 12 weeks. Please submit using our online submission system.

Community Literacy Journal is committed to inclusive citation practices and encourages authors to cite and acknowledge ideas of BIPOC scholars, activists, and organizers in community literacy.

The *Community Literacy Journal* also welcomes shorter manuscripts (10-15 pages) for three sections reviewed in-house:

Community Literacy Project and Program Profiles will discuss innovative and impactful community-based projects and programs that are grounded in best practices.

We encourage community-based practitioners and non-profit staff to submit for this section. Profiles should draw on community literacy scholarship, but they are not expected to have the extended lit reviews that are customary in the articles section of the journal. If you are a community member wanting to submit, and it is your first time writing for an academic journal, we are happy to offer mentorship and answer questions. Pieces co-authored by multiple stakeholders in a project are also welcome.

Please submit using our online submission system. Contact the Project and Program Profiles Editor, Vincent Portillo, with questions at portilvi@bc.edu.

Issues in Community Literacy will offer targeted analysis, reflection, and/or complication of ongoing challenges associated with the work of community literacy. Potential subjects for this section include (but are not limited to): building/sustaining infrastructure, navigating institutional constraints, pursuing community literacy in graduate school, working with vulnerable populations, building ethical relationships, realizing reciprocity, and negotiating conflicts among partners. We imagine this as a space for practitioners to raise critical issues or offer a response to an issue raised in a previous volume of the *CLJ*.

We encourage community-based practitioners and non-profit staff to submit for this section. If you are a community member wanting to submit, and it is your first time writing for an academic journal, we are happy to offer mentorship and answer questions. Pieces co-authored by multiple stakeholders in a project are also welcome.

Please submit using our online submission system. Contact the Issues in Community Literacy Editor, Michelle LaFrance with questions at mlafran2@gmu.edu.

Coda: Community Writing and Creative Work welcomes submissions of poetry, creative nonfiction, short stories, and multi-genre work on any topics that have ensued from community writing projects. This may be work about community writing projects, and this may be expressed in ways we have yet to imagine. We ask authors to include a personal reflection about the submission itself--information about your community writing group (if you belong to one); your personal journey as a writer; what inspired you to write your piece; and anything else you'd care to share about your life--as an invitation for the author and Coda's readers to consider writing and activism as intertwined. Contact Coda Editors with questions at Coda.Editors@gmail.com.

Authors interested in reviewing for the CLJ should contact Book and New Media Review Editor Jessica Shumake at jessica.shumake@gmail.com.

Advertising

Community Literacy Journal welcomes advertising. The journal is published twice annually, in the Fall and Spring (December and June). Deadlines for advertising are two months prior to publication

Ad Sizes and Pricing

Half page (trim size 5.5 x 4.25): $200
Full page (trim size 5.5 x 8.5): $350

Inside back cover (trim size 5.5 x 8.5): $500
Inside front cover (trim size 5.5 x 8.5): $600

Format

We accept .PDF, .JPG, .TIF or .EPS. All advertising images should be camera-ready and have a resolution of 300 dpi. For more information, please contact the journal co-editors at editorsclj@gmail.com.

Copyright © 2024 *Community Literacy Journal*
ISSN 1555-9734

Community Literacy Journal is a member of the Council of Editors of Learned Journals.

Production and distribution managed by Parlor Press.

Publication of the Community Literacy Journal is made possible through the generous support of the University Writing Program at the University of Denver. The CLJ is a journal of the Coalition for Community Writing. Current issues and archives are available open access at https://digitalcommons.fiu.edu/communityliteracy/

Editorial Board

Steven Alvarez, *St. John's University*
Kirk Branch, *Montana State University*
Lisa Dush, *DePaul University*
Paul Feigenbaum, *University at Buffalo*
Jenn Fishman, *Marquette University*
Shirley Brice Heath, *Stanford University*
Glenn Hutchinson, *Florida International University*
Tobi Jacobi, *Colorado State University*
Ben Kuebrich, *West Chester University*
Carmen Kynard, *Texas Christian University*
Paula Mathieu, *Boston College*
Seán Ronan McCarthy, *Montclair University*
Beverly Moss, *The Ohio State University*
Lauren Rosenberg, *University of Texas at El Paso*
Donnie Johnson Sackey, *University of Texas at Austin*
Rachael W. Shah, *University of Nebraska-Lincoln*
Christopher Wilkey, *Northern Kentucky University*

COMMUNITY LITERACY Journal

spring-summer 2025

Editors	Isabel Baca, *The University of Texas at El Paso*
	Libby Catchings, *University of Denver*
	Veronica House, *University of Denver*
	Rebecca Lorimer Leonard, *University of Massachusetts, Amherst*
Acquisitions Editor	Sherita Roundtree, *Towson University*
Issues in Community Literacy Editor	Michelle LaFrance, *George Mason University*
Production Editor and Journal Manager	Walter Lucken IV, *Queens College CUNY*
Book and New Media Review Editor	Jessica Shumake, *University of Notre Dame*
Coda: Community Writing and Creative Work Editorial Collective	Gabrielle Kelenyi, *Lafayette College*
	Chad Seader, *William Penn University*
	Alison Turner, *ACLS Leading Edge Fellow, Jackson, Mississippi*
	Stephanie Wade, *Stony Brook University*
Senior Copyeditor	Elvira Carrizal-Dukes, *University of Texas at El Paso*
Copyeditors	Keshia McClantoc, *University of Nebraska-Lincoln*
	Cayce Wicks, *Florida International University*

community literacy journal

COMMUNITY LITERACY *journal*

Spring-Summer 2025
Volume 19, Issue 2

1 *Editors' Introduction*
   Isabel Baca and Libby Catchings

Articles

3 *"Stacks, Sounds, and a Record a Day": An Introduction to DJ Rhetoric and Sonic Lineage in Praxis*
   Todd Craig

23 *Listening to Black Girls: Community Engaged Considerations of Intellectual Humility*
   Khirsten L. Scott, Elise Silva, Ariana Brazier

49 *Feeling Like a Writer: Composing & Publishing Writer's Memos in a University-Adjacent Writing Group for Low-Income Adults*
   Gabrielle Isabel Kelenyi

Coda: Community Writing and Creative Work

65 *Editors' Introduction: An Alphabet of Resistance*
   Gabrielle Kelenyi, Chad Seader, Alison Turner, and Stephanie Wade

68 *Plantulary*
   Sequoia Hauck, Rachel Jendrzejewski, Koa Mirai, Mankwe Ndosi, Lela Pierce, Pramila Vasudevan, and Jeffrey Wells

73 *Freedom Is Fundamental*
   S. M. Foysol Ahmed, Heather Cleary, and Gwendolyn Hooks

   S. M. Foysol Ahmed
   In the Silence

Heather M. Sloane Cleary
The Assumption
Gwendolyn Hooks
Answers

78 *The Sound You Never Forget*
Ania Payne

82 *Two Poems by Three Authors*
Bonnie Vidrine-Isbell, Aurora Matzke, and Genesea Carter

87 *#WeAllWrite/We All Right*
Tabitha Espina and Kelvin Keown

93 *The Pond*
Joonna Smitherman Trapp

97 *the intersection: Balance of a Wait-less World*
The Moonlight Cheese Alliance and Leslee N. Johnson

101 *How We See Free*
Debbie Allen, Susann Moeller, Chuck Salmons, Rikki Santer, and Karen Scott

110 *The Peach Tree*
Calley Marotta

Book Reviews

115 *From the Book and New Media Review Editor's Desk*
Jessica Shumake, Editor

116 *Community Listening: Stories, Hauntings, Possibilities*
Reviewed by Jennifer W. Grauvogl

122 *Reading, Writing, and Queer Survival: Affects, Matterings, and Literacies Across Appalachia*
Reviewed by Eileen Lagman and Elizabeth Keylon

Editors' Introduction

Isabel Baca and Libby Catchings

We write this introduction at a pivotal time for the *Community Literacy Journal*, welcoming new editors and restructuring our editorial board and the journal itself. As we explore possibilities and opportunities to make *CLJ* more accessible, engaging, and inclusive, we look forward to showcasing intersectional work that represents the varied, multimodal, and often digitally-situated literacies shaping everyday contexts.

As we open this new chapter, we thank the following individuals for their service: Sherita Roundtree (Acquisitions Editor), Natasha N. Jones (Spring General Issues Co-editor), Vincent Portillo (Project Profiles Editor), and Elvira Carrizal-Dukes (Senior Copyeditor). Your thoughtful, behind-the-scenes work has assured the journal's continued success. So, too, do we specially thank Veronica House, *CLJ* co-editor since 2018, for her contributions, vision, and hard work in maintaining the journal and overseeing its production, growth, and success. With our gratitude and excitement, we also welcome our new editorial team members: Libby Catchings (Spring General Issues Co-editor), Jasmine Villa (Project Profiles Editor), and Keshia Mcclantoc (Senior Copyeditor).

The contents of this summer issue reflect different aspects of community listening and community empathy. We begin with Todd Craig's "'Stacks, Sounds and a Record a Day': An Introduction to DJ Rhetoric and Sonic Lineage in Praxis," which emulates sonic argument in a textual medium to revisit the dialogue between hip hop literacies and DJ rhetoric as they shape classroom pedagogies and social change, foregrounding the methodological work of narrative as critical meaning-making practice. Beginning with an origin story that traces the influence of albums, mixtapes, and DJ radio shows on his own identity, Craig guides the reader through the anticipatory logics of the genre's sonic lineage, emphasizing how a DJ's "algorithmic intuition" deploys sampling and interpolation to connect listener to source in ways that build self knowledge. This process of subject formation – what he describes as, "digging in the crates" – mirrors the problem-solving and inductive research students conduct in both scholarship and everyday cultural practice. These sites of literacy, in turn, enable DJ rhetorics to respond to the challenges of anti-black racism and global conflict.

At the same time, Craig's sonic lineage depends on listening that is asynchronous, unidirectional, and citational, even as he stresses the rhetorical nature of how DJs adapt and reconfigure sound by adapting beat and pacing to new contexts (and new compositions). In contrast, our second piece, "Listening to Black Girls: Community Engaged Considerations of Intellectual Humility," narrates a literacy practice centered in synchrony, where justice-centered listening requires both intellectual humility and adaptiveness to community rhythms that aren't always neat or predictable. Where Craig acknowledges the legacy of Black feminist practice to DJ rhetorics as a whole, Khirsten L. Scott, Elise Silva, and Ariana Brazier make Black feminist thought and community listening central to their account of HYPE Media, a community-engaged project in Pittsburgh's Homewood neighborhood that invokes play as a means of resisting the misogynoir and surveillance Black girls experience on a daily basis.

Embodying HYPE Media's emphasis on synchronic dialogue through the polyvocality of the text itself, the authors alternate positionalities to navigate the generational, institutional discourses invoked by community-engaged work in the Homewood community: Scott, the first Black woman in a Rhet-Comp tenure-track position at her R1 institution; Brazier, a Black woman organizer and scholar, and Silva, a white woman in library and information science invested in critical pedagogy.

Gabrielle I. Kelenyi's piece, "Feeling Like a Writer: Composing & Publishing Writer's Memos in a University-Adjacent Writing Group for Low-Income Adults," guides our focus to the less-explored genre of the Writer's Memo in the community publishing context. Using interview data and writer's memo excerpts from a University-Adjacent Writing Group for Low-Income Adults (OWG), Kelenyi demonstrates how the memo as a genre of activity clarifies writers' beliefs, motivations, and sense of self efficacy. Unlike the synchronous spaces of community listening described by Scott et al, Kelenyi's account of writer's memos reveal a dialogue between writer and imagined listener towards each individual's particular (and highly contextual) goals, values, and needs. The resulting dialogue between writer and reader constitutes an adaptive, portable collaboration, not unlike Craig's sonic lineages - each contribution moving towards meaningful negotiation of whose voice gets to be heard.

The Coda: Community Writing and Creative Work section, edited by Gabrielle Kelenyi, Alison Turner, Stephanie Wade, and Chad Seader, begins with the Coda section editors introducing the creative contributions with an Alphabet of Resistance. This alphabet accentuates the language the federal government has removed from their websites and highlights the importance of these words. The contributors in this Coda section provide reflections, poetry, descriptions of visual projects, and even an excerpt of a book in progress.

In the Book and New Media section, edited by Jessica Shumake, you will find two book reviews. Jennifer W. Grauvogl reviews *Community Listening: Stories, Hauntings, Possibilities*, edited by Jenn Fishman, Romeo Garcia, and Lauren Rosenberg. Eileen Lagman and Elizabeth Keylon review *Reading, Writing, and Queer Survival: Affects, Matterings, and Literacies Across Appalachia* by Caleb Pendygraft.

Together – the articles, creative works, and book reviews – create a platform for writing, broadly conceived, and community listening toward greater empathy. We are proud to share this issue with you, our readers, as we welcome new directions for the *Community Literacy Journal*.

Articles

"Stacks, Sounds, and a Record a Day": An Introduction to DJ Rhetoric and Sonic Lineage in Praxis

Todd Craig

Abstract

At the juncture where education meets technology and new media, Hip Hop can serve as one of the most transformative teaching tools. "'Stacks, Sounds and a Record a Day': An Introduction to DJ Rhetoric and Sonic Lineage in Praxis" harnesses this very energy: using personal narrative alongside scholarship in the field of rhetoric and composition, this article surveys a theoretical argument for DJ Rhetoric (Craig 2023) and sonic lineage. These innovative concepts can positively contribute to how we envision writing, rhetoric and the power of the DJ to serve as both cultural educator and changemaker.

Keywords: DJ Rhetoric, Sonic Lineage, Hip Hop Studies, DITC, DJ culture

At the juncture where education meets technology and new media, Hip Hop can serve as one of the most transformative teaching tools. "'Stacks, Sounds and a Record a Day': An Introduction to DJ Rhetoric and Sonic Lineage in Praxis" harnesses this very energy: using personal narrative alongside scholarship in the field of rhetoric and composition, this article surveys a theoretical argument for DJ Rhetoric (Craig 2023) and sonic lineage. These innovative concepts can positively contribute to how we envision writing, rhetoric and the power of the DJ to serve as both cultural educator and changemaker.

"'Stacks, Sounds and a Record a Day': An Introduction to DJ Rhetoric and Sonic Lineage in Praxis" moves similarly to a DJ mix show, down to the layout on the page: you may not know where the DJ is going or what the DJ will play, but you trust in the reputation of the DJ to take you on a sonic expedition. That's why you tune into the show regularly, isn't it? I ask that you walk with me, understanding there is an initial investment to be made in order to fully grasp the gist of this writing experience on the other side of the finish line. I also ask you to walk with me understanding my own reputation. I've been a DJ for over thirty years, and I've been writing about the DJ in academic spaces for over twenty years[1]; thus, I've been a DJ longer than I've been an academic. Furthermore, a significant key to this writing is that the perspective is part of the production; in this moment, my perspective as a DJ drives this conversation on the page.

There are a series of critical commitments this article will address. First – this piece should feel more like a conversation, and less like the "traditional" journal article you might be used to tackling. It will read as a snapshot of persuasive language. Trust me, this idea will come to light by the end of the piece. Second – because this writing aims to further explore and expand upon my previous introduction to DJ Rhetoric, it requires that certain areas are privileged over others. Storytelling is beyond important. In this space, the narrative components are not simply fictional anecdotes; instead, they are meaning-making elements, the skeletal framework that undergirds a theoretical and scholarly conversation. Thus, there is a story to be told by the author, which gives way to how some of the scholarship and theoretical concepts take shape. Furthermore, this storytelling does not wax poetic (although good stories about wax can be quite poetic, but alas, I digress…); it is real-time praxis, connecting the storyteller, the practice(s) of the DJ and how those practices might connect to, disrupt or even reject scholarly sentiments. Essentially, this article does not conform to the conventional paradigm of scholarship as the primary entrée with a story on the side. In *this* moment, the stories *are* the scholarship, the narrative is the archive and how they connect to Hip Hop and DJ culture is canon. Third – and most important – Hip Hop culture is *always* privileged. After all, without Hip Hop music and culture, there would be no narrative to tell. And I argue that without the narrative of Hip Hop culture and the DJ, there is no viable scholarship or sensible theory on this subject. I've now situated how this piece will move. So let's go on a journey in order to witness these concepts in praxis…

"When (T)hey (R)eminisce (O)ver (Y)ou, My God…"
The Reflective Recurrence of Origin aka How I Even Got Here in the First Place

In my early years, like many other kids my age, we worked off of a paradigm called "imagination" when we played. We didn't have "Cookie Swirl C" or "B2Cute Cupcake" or even Renegade and Gittin' Sturdy TikToks that my children now geek over! There was no internet advent for us to model our play after; this could very well mean that I'm pushing way past my youth…but I view it as quite simply, *we* were the model for our own play, and we'd get busy for real. Like most kids my age, I had a solid set of toys, but in other moments, our imaginations would take flight towards other unconscious aspirations.

One of the games I'd play with my cousins, and sometimes even by myself, was this version of school/work/life that was more like reenacting what we thought the adults around us were doing. As I think back, we were playing "adulting": what we envisioned as an adult life with all the perks, but without all the bills and underlying responsibilities. I would normally fall in line with the role of my father figure. All I knew as a child was he worked at a college, he was going to school, and he always dressed top-notch, for real. Now that I'm older, I recognize his work at the college was as director of a few different offices (most notably Financial Aid), his schoolwork was the completion of an MBA, and his clothing game was a straight part-time maneuver at *Lord and Taylor* or *Bloomingdales* – one of those big-name upper-end Manhattan stores that afforded him the discount that made his wardrobe possible.

Similar to him, I envisioned myself studying. There was nothing but textbooks all around and they wound up in the cabinets of the antique buffet in my bedroom. Even though I had my own books, I had already devoured those, a conscious act by both choice and force, because my mom did NOT play that "you gonna stop all schooling and learning when you not in school" mess. So in the summertime, my book game continued, whether I liked it or not. Since I ran through my own books like sprinters at a championship track meet, I'd start running through a collection of my dad's books. I always gravitated to the newer ones, and I can still see a few of those textbooks in my head now. There were a couple of business texts, but my favorite one was the upper level math text. The cover was a light-pale pea soup green – a few shades lighter than the Concepts x New Balance "Tannery" 998 – with red letters and the light grey graph-paper grid on the front. In retrospect, he was probably going to return it to the bookstore; it was most likely an expensive text because it had faint pencil underlines…my play may have jacked that plan up, though.

I'd walk around my bedroom with books under my arm like I was an older kid, going to some sort of important college class. I'd open the book, cracking the freshly uncreased binding, and with a separate notebook on the side, I'd do my best rendition of studying. Some of those pages I'd actually try to read, an endeavor in star-shooting: I'd get some of it, but some stood simply as jargon that, at the time, I thought I'd never be able to distinguish. I'd act like I was studying while the NCAA College basketball games were on; it was always a treat for me to see that navy and orange from Syracuse, even though my favorite was that Go Blue Michigan colorway. I knew I'd go to college, I knew I'd play basketball at Michigan (specifically to have access to the team sneakers since before the BTTYS Dunks and the Air Assaults), and I knew I'd study and obtain an advanced education.

But the thread that tied all of this together was always Hip Hop. On the days I played in my bedroom, the game on TV would be turned down, because a tape from the previous night of Hip Hop with Mr. Magic and Marley Marl or Chuck Chillout or Red Alert was the score of this playtime scene. I listened to the tape and absorbed the soundtrack to the culture that was growing through its adolescence alongside my childhood (Hip Hop was born in August 1973, I was born in April 1974). The last element of this trifecta was the sonics of Hip Hop; there were a slew of books in one cabinet, but on the other side was the stereo and an equal, if not larger, stack of records. I'd listen to the radio, to the tapes I made, to the records that were my uncle's sonic sources for his life as a DJ; they would become the foundation of my understanding of music, and my cousin's understanding of soul in his production career. I'd grow up to buy records on my own, and hone and acquire the taste I had in the sights and sounds of Hip Hop culture.

As time went on, the bare walls in my room would soon be filled with pages from *The Source*, when it still served as that. Das EFX, EPMD's "Business as Usual" and Pete Rock and CL Smooth posters from the "All Souled Out" EP and CD packaging would double as décor…walk through that bedroom today, and some of it has weathered the storm called time. As I grew, the presence of those records were just as integral, if not more so, than the presence of those books. And my physical relationship with both were the same. I would pick up a book, study its cover, look at the table of contents and delve into the writing from page first until page last. In the same way I would pick up an album, stare at the front cover image and imagine why the artist made choices in clothes or pictures, in abstract art or photograph. Then I would put the album on the record player and put the needle on the record while I studied the back credits of the album: song titles, producers, writers, band members, and even sample sources or "interpolation" credits. The equality of these chambers in my youthful understanding is the foundational methodology I bring to my life today. Let's be clear: I can close my eyes and envision the image right now, to this day: books on one side, records on the other side, and a clear visual of a pathway into college.

"The SPINificient Revolution":
Exploring the Idea of DJ Rhetoric

DJ Rhetoric stands as the modes, methodologies and discursive elements of the DJ. What does that even mean? Let's unpack this like DJs rubbing new vinyl on their pants legs to crack open the plastic wrap (#IYKYK)…

At the core of pushing towards a DJ Rhetoric sits a contemporary definition of rhetoric given by Carmen Kynard in her 2008 text, "'The Blues Playingest Dog You Ever Heard of': (Re)positioning Literacy through African American Blues Rhetoric." Illuminating a (re)conception of rhetoric in regards to African American student protest history in the 1960s, Kynard states:

> I am using rhetoric to encompass much more than the art of persuasion and stylised speaking. I mean the qualities of language, both oral and written, through which cultural meanings and histories are communicated and thus, where attitudes towards language and life are central. Rhetoric is, thus, a means of discourse, where what gets said in stories, dance, song, paintings and everyday banter communicates belief systems, social values, a sense of the past, notions of shared identity and communal aspirations. (Kynard 396)

Let's look at another contemporary example to bring this sentiment into focus. On the Griselda Records founder Westside Gunn's 2016 album entitled *Flygod*, the song "Outro" finds Bro. A.A. Rashid talking that talk, and explaining the importance of not compromising one's artistic vision with music, fashion or branding. In this three-minute soliloquy, he hits a very key idea: "You better curate your art, nigguh. You better tell these nigguhs why you do what you do. 'Cause there ain't nobody gonna be there to explain that shit. You need rhetoric! Who told you rhetoric was a bad word? Nigguhs don't read enough! Listen: rhetoric means persuasive language" (Rashid). The culmination of Bro. A. A. Rashid's ruminations in this song connected to the beat speak to both the nexus and expansion of Kynard's analysis. Both Kynard and Rashid are also working to engage with their respective communities. For Kynard, it is an academic audience deeply invested in the educational practices of Black and Brown youth. Meanwhile, Rashid is speaking to a particular slice of the Hip Hop listening community; the placement on Westside Gunn's album automatically targets listeners who appreciate grimy and gritty lyricism, and dark melodic beats. Whether pedestrian or seasoned listeners, this particular sonic community is engaged in "Hip Hop music as strategic curated art." These sounds typically stray from the "Radio Rap Bops" that most people might interact with.

Here, I add onto both Rashid's and Kynard's definitions: part of a DJ's language extends beyond just the "language, oral and written." DJ Rhetoric is also about what gets said "sonically" by a DJ. The ways in which DJs decide to express themselves and communicate that expression amongst members within and outside of DJ culture via turntables and the sounds they create with their arsenal/archive/collection of music has everything to do with the sonic quality of the choices they make (Craig 2023). So a DJ's language progresses beyond just what gets said in songs by an MC or singer, and incorporates the actual sonics of the song; thus, how what gets said in the song coalesces with the music present to make it a complete work. Essentially, it's about how that DJ works and interacts "in the mix" with other pre-fixed songs, or even in the mix by completely (re)configuring pre-fixed songs. And when I say "in the mix" I want to be clear that I mean…mixing songs! The fundamental premise of a DJ blending and beat-matching music based on listening to tempos and pacing of songs and finding clever and seamless ways to manipulate songs to sound fire together, one after the other. For real DJs, "in the mix" is not the artificial DJ pocket, where everyone – they momma, daddy and best friend's cousin's auntie – thinks they can be a DJ. In all honesty, the language of the DJ does not include Broadway theatrics upon entrance to your DJ set. This philosophy is NOT based solely upon a sync button or a mathematical sentiment, or the inability to split double-time numbers into typical BPM representations.[2] We not about that on this side, my friends…

While DJ Rhetoric stands as the modes, methodologies and discursive elements of the DJ, it simultaneously encompasses the quality of oral, written and sonic language that displays and expresses socio-cultural, historical and musical meanings, attitudes and sentiments. From what gets said in the songs to what gets looped in the break in the mix, from the part of the song that gets cut up and scratched on the 1s and 2s. From what gets stretched, rearranged, and completely reorganized as it's coming through your speakers to what gets chopped, screwed and flipped in the sample. From what gets sprayed and laid on the walls in technicolor to what gets captured physically in the ambidextrous movements of all that poppin and lockin, uprockin' and floorwork.

When you start to think about Hip Hop culture, the DJ is the glue: the cornerstone, the conductor, and the connective tissue of the culture as we know it. Because the DJ serves as the catalyst for multiple aspects of rhyming, dance and visual arts coming together and colliding under one roof to form the culture we know as Hip Hop, understanding the modes and techniques of the DJ become paramount in making sense of DJ Rhetoric. If we "dig in the crates" to contemplate the family tree of rhetorical sensibilities surrounding DJ Rhetoric, there is an interconnectedness between Hip Hop rhetoric (and more largely, Hip Hop studies) as well as African American rhetoric. In the same way Hip Hop is rooted in the Black community, so too is the language, discursive practices and techniques of the Hip Hop DJ (Craig

2023). There is a rich and robust history of African American rhetoric – documented in texts that provide both a survey and an examination of the field from its roots to contemporary concepts – from Ronald Jackson and Elaine Richardson's *Understanding African American Rhetoric: Classical Origins to Contemporary Innovations* to Vershawn Young and Michelle Robinson's *The Routledge Reader of African American Rhetoric: The Longue Durée of Black Voices*. There are also studies that illuminate rhetorical contexts in specific community settings, including Vorris L. Nunley's "*Keepin' it Hushed: The Barbershop and African American Hush Harbor Rhetoric*, Mitchell Duneier's *Slim's Table: Race, Respectability, and Masculinity*, and Sacha Jenkins, Elliott Wilson, Gabe Alvarez, and Brent Rollins' *Ego Trip's: Book of Rap Lists*, to name a few. In Jackson and Richardson's seminal text, they envision the major themes of African American rhetoric as "ethics, history, spirituality, language, politics, nationality, religion, gender, popular culture, law, and aesthetics…we define African American rhetoric as it relates to Black African descendants and their experiences in the United States of America" (Jackson and Richardson xiv-xv). Within the realm of African American rhetoric, most people would place Hip Hop rhetoric as a subset of the field. However, I propose a different argument:

> Everyday banter, and thus linguistic directives, for Hip Hop were always communicated in songs, and the banter was a transactional process—a call-and-response of sorts—between the artists and the streets. But the DJs make and break those influential records that begin to dictate the language of the culture. Thus, DJ Rhetoric leads not only to a certain form of DJ Literacy but to a certain form of Hip Hop Language and Literacy (Alim, *Roc the Mic Right*; Richardson, *Hiphop Literacies*) as well. It is here that one could make the argument that HHNL is a submerged area of DJ Rhetoric and Literacy, which is a submerged area of Black Language and rhetoric and African-American literacy. (Craig 58)

Thus, what's critical to keep in mind as we close this rhetoric crate-diggin' session is that DJ Rhetoric stands as the modes, methodologies, and discursive elements of the DJ.

DJ Rhetoric also communicates the values of Hip Hop culture, (re)shaping it as we have known, now know, and will continue to know it. Furthermore, it culminates in a Black space because of how it was birthed and nurtured in urban inner-city Black enclaves. On the one hand, these Black melting pot communities fostered a connectivity between African, African American, Caribbean and Latino/a sentiments. These very Black locations were landmark communities established as post-white-flight stomping grounds. So there were mad Black folx all around, playing various iterations of Black music. These Black stylings were housed in Black city sites:

> By the end of the decade, half of the whites were gone from the South Bronx. They moved north to the wide-open spaces of Westchester County or the northeastern reaches of Bronx County…white elite retrenchment found a violent counterpart in the browning streets. When African-American, Afro-Caribbean, and Latino families moved into formerly Jewish, Irish, and

Italian neighborhoods, white youth gangs preyed on the new arrivals in schoolyard beatdowns and running street battles" (Chang 12).

Out of these geographic spaces abandoned by whites and newly occupied by various people of the Black diaspora, Hip Hop is born. And the attending physician who promotes pushing between contractions is the DJ.

I Wrote This to the "Terry" Beat on Repeat aka "…Virgil Abloh throw rug to roll you up like Fruit Roll-Up…" aka The Lineage Called DJ Rhetoric

I remember sharing the childhood story from two sections ago with my homie Dr. Bilal Polson as I unknowingly took a roughly eight-mile walk in the summer of 2019. I was trooping it from dropping my car off for service at the dealership in Jersey City; I tried to make my way back to Weehawken, and I got a good halfway before I recognized that Nike Slides are *not* the shoe of choice for such endeavors. However, the extended walk gave me the time I needed to chop it up with Bilal. In these early conversations, we would discuss how our sonic sensibilities informed, influenced, and infused how we moved through our roles as educators, our notions of pedagogy, but also how those two elements could inform and influence how we guided public conversations around music – for both the academy and the students we teach. I remember this moment clearly, as it would spark a number of theories for both of us. This dual-layered narrative is critically important to how the idea of sonic lineage (Polson) was sparked. My conversation with Bilal about this moment was one he told me I would need to share. Bilal and I build consistently on Hip Hop music, culture and its relevance to teaching and learning from K-16. This narrative was part of our convo that took myriad twists and turns. As Principal of an elementary school, Polson uses Hip Hop as a catalyst for how students engage in art, music and English Language Arts (ELA) classes. For me, I was thinking through teaching a new class at City Tech for the African American Studies Department entitled "Hip-Hop Worldview" – for this class, I was specifically ruminating on how Rapsody's *Eve* album could connect students to Hip Hop's past, present and future, thus connecting them into multigenerational Hip Hop conversations.[3] While doing this thinking, I was also solidifying the revisions for my full-length manuscript that revolved around DJ Rhetoric, literacy and pedagogy. At the time of this conversation, I was wading through the turbulent waters of just losing my mother. When I received the call to teach the class, I almost didn't accept it. Bilal helped me recognize that my mom's passing and the call from Dr. Monique Ferrell to teach the class were not two unconnected pieces of a time-space continuum.

Instead, it was *Kairos*.
Being in the right space and place at the absolute right time…

My mom passed on Saturday, July 27, 2019. I was asked to teach the class two days later, on Monday, July 29, 2019. Thanks, Mommy…

For Dr. Polson, Principal of Northern Parkway Elementary School, this conversation was one of the very last moments before he launched his multimedia "#literacylives #textual-lineage" project. These collective think-tank build-sessions ultimately led to the concept of sonic lineage. Let's unpack these terms and definitions to determine how DJ Rhetoric and sonic lineage become an integral addition to the 21st century parameters of Hip Hop studies, and Rhetoric and Composition.

DJ Rhetoric, "Digging in the Crates" and the Bridge to Textual Lineage

The art of understanding records through the timeless tradition of "digging in the crates" (also known as DITC) is part of the apprenticeship that all DJs should know. While many DJs transition into being producers (Schloss; Craig [2013, 2015]), they will tell you that solid DJ training has opened the door for them to become greater producers. Within DJ communities and embedded in the trajectory of DJ experiential learning, many DJs carried record crates for other DJs. Part of the experience of carrying crates is learning what those crates contain.

"Digging in the Crates" (DITC) is without question a research methodology that every great DJ has engaged in throughout their career (Craig 2015). A term originally coined by the Bronx crew of rappers, DJs and producers[4] in 1992 (Pizzo), it is a concept that is closely aligned with Lynnée Denise's idea of "DJ Scholarship." DITC is a specific form of DJ research (Denise), connecting a DJ to how they consume, archive and interface with sonic sources (Craig 2023). Many times, the act of "digging" not only involved having a sense of what songs are on a record or what the record looks like visually (from the cover to the actual label on the record), but also studying the liner notes – a distinctive form of writing, rhetoric and early Hip Hop documentation and communication (Coleman): what are some of the key samples; what artists appear on the records; where have you seen and heard those artists before? Daphne A. Brooks keenly assesses the gravitas that liner notes hold in music's sonic cultural education:

> liner notes hold out the possibility of operating as critical, fictional, or experimental works of writing in and of themselves. Conventional liner notes often walk a fine line between pedagogy and socialization, between sociohistorical and cultural reportage and heuristic conditioning (here's how and why to love the artist in question). The most ambitious notes strive toward the narrative realization, or the narrative reimagining, of a sonic collection of songs altogether. And there was a time when the notes had the potential to shore up the supposed import and ambition of a recording, amplifying its intellectual resonance by *writing* its value into the cultural imaginary. (Brooks 5-6)

The composing practices as well as the rhetorical strategies in this moment align with an acute linkage to the concept of textual lineage.

In his 2009 book entitled *Reading for Their Life: (Re)Building the Textual Lineages of African American Adolescent Males,* Alfred Tatum argues that one way to reinvigorate and re-engage African American adolescent males in the subjects of reading and writing is to help them understand their "textual lineage." Tatum describes the idea of a textual lineage as: "similar to lineages in genealogical studies, [textual lineage] is made up of texts (both literary and nonliterary) that are instrumental in one's human development because of the meaning and significance one has garnered from them" (Tatum xiv). Thus, textual lineage can be comprised of authors of importance to the student; as students see the value in the authors they choose, this should translate into an eagerness to read and explore more literature of varying authors, especially if the authors write similar work or come from a similar background or tradition to some of the authors originally presented in a student's textual lineage.

Another way to envision the process is the following: think about the last time you were on *Amazon.com.* If you type in the title *Hip Hop Literacies* (2006) by Dr. Elaine Richardson, you will find all the info pertaining to Dr. E's work. Scroll down the screen and you will find the following section: "Customers who viewed this item also viewed: *Book of Rhymes: The Poetics of Hip Hop* (2009) by Adam Bradley, *Check It While I Wreck It: Black Womanhood, Hip Hop Culture and the Public Sphere* (2004) by Gwendolyn Pough and *African American Literacies* (2002) by Elaine Richardson." Clicking on Dr. Pough's book brings us to a note that says "Frequently Bought Together" which lists the two other books most purchased with *Check It While I Wreck It.* And right underneath that, you can find a list of items that were purchased with Dr. Pough's book, including Tricia Rose's seminal text *Black Noise* (1994), *Can't Stop, Won't Stop* (2005) by Jeff Chang and *Prophets of the Hood* (2004) by Imani Perry. These different lists represent a similar bloodline that comes with particular books…a lineage of sorts. And this lineage can shift and change, based on customer reading choices and purchases. We see this all day long on Amazon, and also on Netflix: if you like *Pulp Fiction* (1994), then you'll LOVE *The Killer* (1989) by John Woo, *City of God* (2002) by Katia Lund, *Snatch* (2000) by Guy Ritchie and *Lucky Number Slevin* (2006) by Paul McGuigan. We also see these machinations musically. If you look back a few sections, you'll remember the story about how I studied records and albums similarly to studying books. Consuming the information on the "mechanics" of the music I loved and listened to allowed me to build a sonic archive, a deep cerebral musical database that connected me to various rifts, sounds and samples when I would hear them in various moments. As I studied the sights, sites, and sounds of my favorite artists and albums (and even the albums that weren't that great), I became steeped in a musical knowledge that you can only acquire by doing listening laps in a sonic swimming pool! This is the work that DJs have always done, and this is what brings the richness of sounds and genre inclusion into Hip Hop's landscape.

As always, feel free to thank your favorite DJ…

Part of any great DJs' philosophical DNA comes from their algorithmic intuition; their ability to isolate, identify and quantify a sonic source, and then build upon it with choices dictated by the sonic choice that first sparked such thinking. This intuition is inherited through learning and steeped in years of listening...

"It ain't what I'm drivin', it's what's drivin' me..." aka "It's a Dirty Game..." aka Doin' the Knowledge on DJ Algorithmic Connections

Let's think back to the narrative I shared about my upbringing. In the same way that perusing and admiring books captured a contextual understanding based on the physical text, listening to albums and mixtapes of DJ radio shows enabled the visual and aural connections I would later understand as tangible connections to how I "see" and "hear" sonic sources. Hence, a certain sound or image might trigger a recollection that brings me back to a particular song, and the moment(s) that song evokes, alongside how I might imagine other songs that are important to the initial sound's trajectory; this triggering alongside this imagining are critical aspects of a human DJ's algorithmic intuition. Thus, a particular type of
"sonic lineage"
furthers a human DJ's algorithmic intuition, as it connects
the physical and aural (or audio) of records and songs
in the same way a book captures a physical context.

It's important to note that when I say "DJ algorithmic intuition," I am also clear about the current use of the term "algorithm." So let's contextualize this quandary with a full understanding and acknowledgement of the racist and discriminatory practices that have come to light when thinking about how contemporary algorithms work based on silent programmer bias (Benjamin 2019; Noble 2018). Ruha Benjamin's work is insightful here, when thinking about how we envision algorithms in our understanding of 21st century digital practices. She states "problem solving is at the heart of tech. An algorithm, after all, is a set of instructions, rules and calculations designed to solve problems...thus, even just deciding *what problem* needs solving requires a host of judgments" (Benjamin 11).

Here, Benjamin helps us to (re)think the problem that Hip Hop would originally aim to solve: extending "the funky part" of any given record. However, because of two of the philosophies of Hip Hop (shared from the Nation of Gods and Earths) – "show and prove" as well as having "knowledge of self" – DJs were not only trying to find "the funky part" of the break, but there's also an acute element of hearing a song today and being able to identify the sample and the original source. For example, sitting at the dinner table a few nights ago with my wife, she was playing soundsmith and curating our sonic dining experience. As soon as Yuna's "Broke Her" started playing, my brain immediately went to Drake's "0 to 100." But to insure I did the proper knowledge, a search quickly found that Frank Dukes aka Adam Feeney produced a beat called "Vibez" (with Chester Stone Hansen) that *both* Yuna and Drake used: Yuna sang over the original beat, then Boi Wonda sampled "the funky part" for the major melody of "0 to 100." Connecting the dots for understanding these sources is not only engaging with the "rules and calculations designed to solve problems" that

Benjamin presents, but it is also a research practice in itself: reviewing the credits and linear notes of a song illustrate a timeline as well as a sonic chronology for how songs that sample other songs line up. It's the type of investigation and exploration we ask of our students in classrooms each and every day – to flesh out an idea with data points and other information available to how we might truly gain a sense of what the current landscape is when thinking through a conversation in progress about an idea that sparks one's thinking. Who thought about it first? Who added on to the concept, or stopped to refute the idea? But most importantly, *what problem needs solving* – what elements have not been interrogated in a way that bring forth new perspectives and knowledge. This is a small glimpse into the DJ algorithmic mindset that solid DJs bring to the table. The DJ's sonic capacity to hear and identify a source and then do the due diligence to understand the song's trajectory is another aspect of sonic lineage. It runs parallel to Denise's other facets of DJ scholarship, specifically the cultural practices she identifies as "chasing samples" and "reading liner notes" (Denise 64). But it also directly speaks to research required of DJs not only wanting to understand "the funky part" of the record, but also needing to know the entire record in order to fit it into a DJ set properly. Much of the musical understanding from early DJs comes from the legacy of the feminist practices that mothers and aunties exhibited with Hip Hop pioneering DJs when they were children (Stoever). Knowing the entire record as well as "the funky part" that served as the groove to those early Park Jams evolved into the grooves that DJs would sample to produce recorded Hip Hop tracks. On the "Geto Boys Reloaded" podcast, Hip Hop DJ, producer, emcee and cultural stalwart Large Professor identifies the bridge between early Hip Hop records and the sources from which they originated, when he states "So when Hip Hop came around…you hear a Grandmaster Flash record, and then now you go in your parents' records and you hear the record that they used and it's like 'oh, this is what they doin'?!? Oh, okay.' Then, now you get out there and start getting with the elders. Like my man in the BX, my man Sgt. Len Funk, he used to put me onto mad records, and give me the stores to go get them. So it was just that community thing, and you have different versions of it" (Large Professor).

Spotify, Pandora and Tidal amongst other streaming services, all operate with a lineage-like algorithm that has changed how newer Hip Hop artists may make music. But it is the DJ, steeped in the listening and reading traditions shared by Black women, who is notorious for helping the listener to connect to songs – sonic sources – they may or may not know of, but fall into place when curating a "soundline," or a sonic lineage. It's not only a list of sources that share the same sentiment, but in some cases, it's an earlier source that predicates the existence of the newer source. It's the lineage, the bloodline, and the family tree. This sentiment is expressed well by DJ Skeme Richards, who recently served as music curator for Red Bull's 2022 BC 1 World Finals. In describing his work as a DJ for Red Bull's global Breaking Competition (BC), Skeme says:

"DJing for me means life. Right? It's culture. The DJ's job is to educate the listener. It's always an educational process. And for me being able to share what I grew up on culturally to the rest of the world, that's so valuable. Because the point of culture – and *this* culture – is lineage, right? And I'm here to pass down that lineage. So my process with getting music together is basically going through a catalogue of music and understanding what works, what doesn't work. Oh, this is BC1, so I need *this* style of music…I walk away from every party after seeing the floor and everybody moving with a smile on my face. Because at the end of the day, I'm like 'I did that.' I brought culture to this space." (Skeme Richards)

It's that DJ algorithmic mindset that initiates the auditory understanding and connections of a sonic lineage. So when my man Carlos of Classic Material New York (CMNY) put me onto Griselda (Craig 2022), I could immediately connect with Mobb Deep, Wu-Tang, G-Unit, Odd Future and other groups of the past that influenced their sonics. My wife's sharing of Yuna brought us to Drake but also to Frank Dukes in the same way my man Chenjerai's recommendation of Oh No brought me to Cue Records and Stone's Throw (and a 20+ year union and partnership). So when Large Professor realized that "Paid in Full" sampled "Ashley's Roachclip" by the Soul Searchers, it was his DJ algorithmic mindset that led him to the Music Factory record store to find the original record (courtesy of Mr. Walt of the Beatminerz). In the same way I recently heard "Looking for the Perfect Beat" and when Bam says "It's Working!" it brought me *right* back to DJ Double K in *Beat Street* (1984). Since Hip Hop's inception, DJs have always held the responsibility of diggin' in the crates to exhibit a specific type of sonic lineage in both theory (with how said DJ connects to and understands the fundamentals of Hip Hop cultural sonic traditions) but also in practice (whether it's sharing those sonic sentiments in a jam, a live event [Weheliye] or even in producing compositions for emcees and vocalists). Much of Hip Hop's sonics went from the Park Jams and the tapes of the Park Jams, to hearing production on songs to chasing down the original records used in the samples (which originally started as the "foundation breaks" – the breaks used at the Park Jams [(Flores in Craig 44]).

DJs brought DITC to life, but the research-minded aspect of the DJ births
a specific desire to acquire a type of
sonic lineage.
These sonic markers spark an intellectual quest
based on narrative and memories soaked in sound.

"Sampling the Sample to Expand the Source": From Textual Lineage to Sonic Lineage

In harnessing the nature and relevance of textual lineage, imagine how powerful Tatum's thinking might be when opened up to a chamber that really felt like a rhetorical strategy when aligned with the DJ. For example, if we push Tatum's philosophy further, and replace the notion of traditional-based "text" with the idea of twenty-first century text – which includes sound, or the sonic, as text – how, then, would "sonic lineage" work? It functions based on the visual language cues and aural rhetoric, the sights, sites, and sounds that inform how one engages with historical musical trajectories, as well as ways that "readers" (or listeners) engage in the learning that comes from the sonic. We can hear this sentiment expressed by Large Professor:

> Even in like the mid 80's and late 80's, there's always gonna be the "Old School-New School" type thing. But at that time, we were the new school now. And the old school dudes knew all the breaks and the beats…now it was coming into a time where there were standard breaks you were supposed to know and you were supposed to have: "Impeach the President," things like that. Like "Substitution", "Kool is Back" by Funk Inc…that piqued [dudes like me and Pete Rock's] interest into like "yo, let's git into these other records now." (Large Professor)

In this moment, Large Pro is tapping into an aural genealogy of sorts – this is the essence of sonic lineage. Again, as DJs isolate mental associations with the visuals of records (from the physical label on the record to the images on the record covers), delve into research practices by consuming liner notes, study every nook and cranny of a record for sound, and discern which record makes sense to play at what time, there are kinesthetic connections based in felt sense that are markers of time and space based in the sonic enterprise…or simply put – memories soaked in sound. Go no further than three sections prior, and you'll see this idea in praxis: the "Terry" beat and "Chopstick" will always be sonic markers for the lineage of this piece.[5]

Another example that might epitomize this work can be found with the path Polson created with his "Literacy Lineage" movement (#literacylives, #textual-lineage). On August 12, 2019 – the day after Hip Hop culture's birthday – Polson started the literacy lineage conversation with what many consider to be the centerpiece of Hip Hop music and production: "Funky Drummer (Part 1)" by James Brown (Polson 2019). From there, on a daily basis, you could find a Tweet, an Instagram post and a Facebook link to a picture of the record label. Sometimes it was an image of the 12", sometimes it was the 45. But for over a year, Polson brought this work to the forefront and continued to push the envelope for what we might consider twenty-first century literacy practices…and all by posting a record a day! I'll admit here, my favorite posts came from the politically-inspired daily entries: for example, the January 13, 2021 entry came from the Honeydrippers. The title…"Impeach the President." On January 7, 2021, the song was "Wake Up Everybody Pt. 1" by Harold Melvin and the Blue Notes. On January 6, 2021…"Midnight Train to Georgia" by Gladys Knight and the Pips. And finally, on January 19, 2021: "Hit the Road Jack."

What is most impressive about this initiative is Polson isn't qualifying, quantifying or making any judgments, value claims or even assessments of the records he chooses daily. Instead, it's simply about the label of the record or the 45 – the visual – that opens the door for *other people* to begin to document their own narratives around the influence and importance of the song. He isn't assessing, he's merely serving as a selector: facilitating a digital space for a community of readers/listeners to engage in memories (visual and sonic), thinking and theories on the importance of each sonic text the daily post highlights. Here, Polson fills a void and solves the problem of creating the space for sonic reflection and memory, while also bringing us back to foundational sonic elements of Hip Hop culture that demand reflection and require review and recollection for the upcoming generation of Hip Hop scholars and cultural practitioners. Polson is also operating in a way that aligns with D. Bruce Campbell Jr.'s theory of cultural citation; Polson's IG posts embody story sharing as "an individual that is embedded in that culture or better yet, present for the story they are sharing" (Campbell 46). Polson is not only sharing sonic markers that initiate the storytelling of various Hip Hop cultural participants, but he himself is present, embedded in the culture and present for the story being shared; this allows for both authentic storytelling and accurate, sharable (and fact-checkable) narrative experiences. Similar to what scholars are doing with genealogy studies, Polson is creating a space for research connections. He is not only building connective webs of family trees for Hip Hop sonic sentiments, but he is also reinforcing the ways in which Hip Hop facilitates a review of the culture's canon; appreciating the original "foundation breaks" (Flores in Craig 44) played at Park Jams, or comprehending how certain R & B songs incite particular Hip Hop centered moments and memories brings a younger generation of Hip Hop heads into bridging their histories with their presence in order to inform their future.

How Might Sonic Lineage Interface With DJ Rhetoric?

So why are sonic lineage and DJ Rhetoric important? Let's put these ideas
in the mix with one another
to see how they blend, like beatmatching two records...

If we understand sonic lineage and DJ Rhetoric as part of a larger scholarly tradition around Hip Hop studies, and its potential within Rhetoric and Composition, and then more broadly still around African American rhetoric, language and literacy, then we can begin to situate the importance of these two particular constructs in the midst of contemporary uprisings and global pandemics.

There is no argument on Hip Hop as global popular culture anymore; it is a given, clear as day, when you turn on the TV and are sold products via Hip Hop in commercials. Take, for example, the pandemic's global DJ: D-Nice, who has parlayed the soul saving sounds of his IG-platform "Club Quarantine" into his own Ford F-150 advertisement, with a score straight outta 1989 with his chart-topping Hip Hop classic "Call Me D-Nice." D-Nice was one of the key DJs who brought us joy and escape in the midst of the earliest grips of the Covid-19 pandemic. His marathon-long IG DJ sets, entitled "Homeschool at Club Quarantine," grew virally to over 100,000 viewers and listeners (Schatz). "Homeschool at Club Quarantine" served as a digital party location that allowed co-workers from a small college to connect virtually on one side of the club, while Michelle Obama, Mark Zuckerberg, Oprah Winfrey, Bernie Sanders and Janet Jackson would slide through on the other; this party created much-needed community, a space for people to engage in a phenomenon of healing, homage and release. It honestly isn't even worth it to argue that Hip Hop is anything *other than* global Black popular culture. It is a given – clear as day – and tangibly actualized when your children turn on their iPads and other devices, and TikTok their way into

Hip Hop centered Black excellence (I'm especially intrigued by the #BlackGirlMagic that comes from Jalaiah Harmon and the Renegade [Lorenz])[6]. As we continue on within a twenty-first century that has centered Hip Hop as the driving force of global popular culture, it is key to understand the value Hip Hop has in its uncanny ability to touch the masses. Hip Hop's cultural capital can be harnessed as a means by which a diverse group of participants can be engaged; such engagement and interaction can be critical, especially in times of socio-political unrest as well as public health crises.

The power of Hip Hop pedagogy is both vast and significant; the ability to (re)imagine a diversity of thought, equity in knowledge sharing and educational practices for both teaching and learning with Hip Hop at the core is far from the "dying fad" the culture was labeled as over fifty years ago.

DJ Rhetoric and sonic lineage can become powerful rhetorical tools when aligned with the National Council of Teachers of English/Conference on College Composition and Communication (NCTE/CCCC) clarion call from 2020, entitled "This Ain't Another Statement! This is a DEMAND for Black Linguistic Justice!". In this statement around the ideas of promoting, proliferating and liberating Black linguistic strategies and rhetorical practices, there is a clear call to acknowledge the brilliance of Black youth and Black language by thwarting anti-Black racist language practices. This call becomes critically important, as we align Black language and linguistic practices with African American rhetoric, DJ Rhetoric and Hip Hop rhetoric. In the same way textual lineage can serve as a roadmap for creating a text-based family tree, I contend that sonic lineage can serve as Hip Hop's auditory family tree, and can contribute to DJ Rhetoric flourishing – as the modes, practices and techniques of the Hip Hop DJ form both a new media conception of sonic writing and the sentiments that sit at the foundation of Hip Hop rhetorical and linguistic practices. Hip Hop's cultural practices did not proliferate themselves through the guise of the emcee; they, instead, did so through the lens of the DJ. Identifying and honoring this historical and sonic lineage sits at the very core of understanding how DJ Rhetoric should be viewed as a creative cornerstone of Hip Hop musical and cultural history.

BONUS BEATS ALERT…
Aka Needle Droppin' Our Way into the Origins of DJ Rhetoric and Sonic Lineage:
How We Might Move Forward

The stacks of records I depicted in the introductory narrative of this article served the same purpose as the stacks I moved through in the Sawyer library, through that big building on Appian Way, and through the last building that housed my doctoral cubicle. These stacks were a culmination of a dream I couldn't really envision detail-wise when I was "adulting" as a child. Still, I knew it would somehow be part of the mission and part of my journey. The idea of holding the cover, reviewing the imagery, squinting at the liner notes, and gaining a sense of the ingredients necessary to cook up each and every one of those albums in and of itself is a form of *and* formal literacy; a way by which the reader can begin to decipher the rhetorical elements of sonic composing. This becomes evident in both volumes of *Check the Technique* by Brian Coleman, which demonstrates the importance of those notes alongside the mental processes explained by the sonic authors we know as Hip Hop artists – deejays and emcees, beatmakers and producers. Visualizing literacy and rhetorical strategies in the twenty-first century has shifted us outside of the typical box presented by "text-based" practices that only transpire on the page. Opening the door to twenty-first century communicative practices such as DJ Rhetoric and sonic lineage can really push the fields of Hip Hop studies as well as Rhetoric and Composition to move towards achieving the demands outlined by the 2020 CCCC Special Committee on Composing a CCCC Statement on Anti-Black Racism and Black Linguistic Justice, Or, Why We Cain't Breathe! in their most recent statement.

At the crossroads where the CCCC Black Linguistic Justice statement, Polson's #literacy-lineage project, DJ Rhetoric and sonic lineage converge is a fruitful location for how we might move forward (re)envisioning the importance of the sonic and the unwritten yet very tangible rhetorical and composing savvy of the DJ – even when the "writing" we may attribute to it is sonic in nature. It is a (re)visioning that could be quite useful for our students, who are connecting and engaging in their lives with the sonic as the score and the backdrop…

one record at a time.

Acknowledgments

Special shout out to c2c, my #WordGameCrew, who's better than yours: Jenny and Inés and Priscilla, what it do!

Notes

1. If you're new to this work, I urge you to keep reading. In the meantime, if you'd like to read more of the scholarship I've written about the DJ in Writing Studies, you can tap into the "Todd Craig" section of the Works Cited page, as well as articles such as ""Heavy Airplay, All Day with No Chorus": Classroom Sonic Consciousness in the Playlist Project" and "Sista Girl Rock: Women of Colour and Hip-Hop Deejaying as Raced/Gendered Knowledge and Language" by myself and Carmen Kynard, just to name a few more.

2. This sentiment is exemplified by Grimes DJ set at Coachella in 2024.

3. I delve into this work deeply in a book chapter entitled "'How Eve Saved My Soul': Sonic Lineage as the Prequel to the Playlist Project."

4. D.I.T.C. as a Hip Hop crew consists of Lord Finesse, Diamond D, Show (formally known as Showbiz), A.G., Fat Joe, O.C., Buckwild, and Big L (RIP). They originally coined this term as a crew name, Diggin' In The Crates, but also to describe the act of mining for samples and extensive record-shopping missions. It is important to credit this crew of Hip Hop cultural practitioners for the work they've done in giving the world this term.

5. What up, ALC? Typically, I call him Al. You might call him The Alchemist…

6. Shout out to Jalailah as the original Renegader (you can tap in to what she's doing on IG at @jalaiah). Hopefully this citation helps to document her pioneering creative status; this is my attempt to highlight her #BlackGirlMagic and not allow this to become the next Harlem Shake moment.

Works Cited

Action Bronson, vocal performance of "Terry," by Action Bronson, on *Mr. Wonderful*, Atlantic/Vice, 2015. MP3.

Afrika Bambaataa and Soulsonic Force, vocal performance of "Looking for the Perfect Beat," by Afrika Bambaataa and Soulsonic Force, on *Planet Rock: The Album*, Tommy Boy/Warner Bros. 1986. Vinyl.

Atcoates. "Beat Street Double K gets the party started. (new 480p version)," Youtube, June 29, 2010, video, 2:55, https://www.youtube.com/watch?v=55PwRz_HwmY.

Baker-Bell, April, Bonnie Williams-Farrier, Davena Jackson, Lamar Johnson, Carmen Kynard, and Teaira McMurtry. "This Ain't Another Statement! This Is a DEMAND for Black Linguistic Justice!" Conference on College Composition and Communication, August 3, 2020. https://cccc.ncte.org/cccc/demand-for-black-linguistic-justice.

Benjamin, Ruha. *Race After Technology*. Cambridge: Polity, 2019.

Bro. A. A. Rashid, vocal performance of "Outro," by Bro. A. A. Rashid and Westside Gunn, on *Flygod*, Griselda Records, 2016. MP3.

Brooks, Daphne A. *Liner Notes for the Revolution: The Intellectual Life of Black Feminist Sound*. Cambridge: The Belknap Press of Harvard University Press, 2021.

Campbell, D. Bruce, Jr. "Cultivating a Rebel Without a Pause." *Essays on Music, Adolescence, and Identity: The Adolescentia Project*. Edited by M.B. Ray, 45-56. Switzerland: Palgrave Macmillan, 2024.

Chang, Jeff. *Can't Stop Won't Stop: A History of the Hip Hop Generation*. New York: Picador, 2005.

Coleman, Brian. *Check the Technique: Liner Notes for Hip-Hop Junkies*. New York: Villard, 2009.

Coleman, Brian. *Check the Technique Volume 2: More Liner Notes for Hip-Hop Junkies*. Everett: Wax Facts Press, 2014.

Craig, Todd. "'Jackin' for Beats': DJing for Citation Critique." *Radical Teacher* 97 (2013): 20-29.

—. *K for the Way: DJ Rhetoric and Literacy for 21st Century Writing Studies*. Logan: Utah State University Press, 2023.

—. "'Makin' Somethin' Outta Little-to-Nufin'': Racism, Revision and Rotating Records–The Hip-Hop DJ in Composition Praxis." *Changing English* 22, no. 4 (2015): 349-364.

—. "'Tell Virgil Write BRICK on my brick': Doctoral Bashments, (Re)Visiting Hiphopography and the Digital Discursivity of the DJ: A Mixed Down Methods Movement." In *Methods and Methodologies for Research in Digital Writing and Rhetoric*

Centering Positionality in Computers and Writing Scholarship, Volume 1. Edited by Crystal VanKooten and Victor Del Hierro, 87-107. Fort Collins: WAC Clearinghouse, 2022.

—. "'The Breaks, The Archives and the OG Algorithm': The DJ as the Connective Healer and Curatorial Cornerstone–A Selected Experience." *The Bloomsbury Handbook of Hip Hop Pedagogy*. Edited by Lauren Leigh Kelley and Daren Graves, 38-47. New York: Bloomsbury, 2024.

D-Nice. "The All-New 2021 F-150: Work It Out," YouTube, February 6, 2021, video, 0:35, https://www.youtube.com/watch?v=PshfTINkTNM&feature=youtu.be

Denise, Lynnée D. "The Afterlife of Aretha Franklin's 'Rock Steady': A Case Study in DJ Scholarship." *The Black Scholar 49*, no. 3 (2019): 62-72.

Drake, vocal performance of "0 to 100/ The Catch Up" by Drake, Young Money/Cash Money/Republic Records, 2014.

Duneier, Mitchell. *Slim's Table: Race, Respectability, and Masculinity*. Chicago: University of Chicago Press, 2015.

Feeney, Adam. *Vibez*. With Chester Stone Hansen. Kingsway Music Library. March 4, 2015. MP3, 3:25, https://soundcloud.com/liteeaseradio/adam-feeney-vibez.

Jackson II, Ronald L., and Elaine B. Richardson, eds. *Understanding African American Rhetoric: Classical Origins to Contemporary Innovations*. New York: Routledge, 2003.

Jenkins, Sacha, Elliott Wilson, Gabe Alvarez, and Brent Rollins. *Ego Trip's: Book of Rap Lists*. New York: Macmillan, 1999.

Kynard, Carmen. "'The Blues Playingest Dog You Ever Heard Of': (Re)positioning Literacy Through African American Blues Rhetoric." *Reading Research Quarterly* 43, no. 4 (2008): 356-373.

Large Professor. "Ultimate Breaks and Beats Influence on Me and Hip Hop." 247HH.COM, video, July 2, 2017, https://www.youtube.com/watch?v=HpiluShMexU&t=119s.

—. "Large Professor On Roots of Hip Hop Prod, CORPORATE-TAKEOVER of the Culture; Talks G Rap, Nas and More." Geto Boys Reloaded, video, November 5, 2022, https://www.youtube.com/watch?v=73MjSto2VAg.

Lorenz, Taylor. "The Original Renegade." *The New York Times*. February 13, 2020. https://www.nytimes.com/2020/02/13/style/the-original-renegade.html.

Noble, Safiya Umoja. *Algorithms of Oppression: How Search Engines Reinforce Racism*. New York: New York University Press, 2018.

Nunley, Vorris L. *Keepin' it Hushed: The Barbershop and African American Hush Harbor Rhetoric*. Detroit: Wayne State University Press, 2011.

Pete Rock and C.L. Smooth, vocal performance of "They Reminisce Over You (T.R.O.Y.)," by Pete Rock and C.L. Smooth, on *Mecca and the Soul Brother*, Untouchables/Elektra, 1992. Vinyl.

Pizzo, Mike. "Still Diggin': An Oral History of D.I.T.C." Medium. May 11, 2016. https://medium.com/cuepoint/still-diggin-an-oral-history-of-d-i-t-c-b91d44360a8e

Polson, Bilal. "Breaking Through: Dr. Bilal Polson on Music, Mentorship & Leading with Purpose." The Breakthrough Collective, video, August, 21, 2025, https://www.youtube.com/watch?v=bzA75pAjWsI.

—. "Literacy-lineage: #literacy #literacylives #textual-lineage #HitTheRoadJack #RayCharles #PercyMayfield #AlfredTatum" Instagram, January 19, 2021. Access date February 1, 2021. https://www.instagram.com/p/CKOCwjvhqU7/.

—. "Literacy-lineage: #literacy #literacylives #textual-lineage #JamesBrown #AlfredTatum." Instagram, August 12, 2019. Access date July 21, 2020. https://www.instagram.com/p/B1D_wLxgvf1/.

—. "Literacy-lineage: #literacy #literacylives #textual-lineage #ImpeachThePresident #TheHoneyDrippers #RoyCHammond #AlfredTatum." Instagram, January 13, 2021. Access date February 1, 2021. https://www.instagram.com/p/CJ_x5Kdh3kH/.

—. "Literacy-lineage: #literacy #literacylives #textual-lineage #WakeUpEverybody #HaroldMelvin&TheBlueNotes #HaroldMelvin. #BernardWilliams #RooseveltBrodie #JesseGillisJr #FranklinPeaker #JohnAtkins #TeddyPendergrass #LawrenceBrown #JohnWhitehead #GeneMcFadden #VictorCarstarphen #AlfredTatum @realsway @thehappyhourwhb." Instagram, January 7, 2021. Access date February 1, 2021. https://www.instagram.com/p/CJvwhufh17A/.

—. "Literacy-lineage: #literacy #literacylives #textual-lineage #MidnightTraintoGeorgia #GladysKnightAndThePips #JimWeatherly #AlfredTatum." Instagram, January 6, 2021. Access date February 1, 2021. https://www.instagram.com/p/CJsk45dB9Jt/.

Roc Marciano and The Alchemist. "Chopstick." *Skeleton Key*. Pimpire/ALC Records, 2024. Tidal.

—. "Skirt Steak." *Skeleton Key*. Pimpire/ALC Records, 2024. Tidal.

Schatz, Lake. "D-Nice is Throwing the Most Lit, Star-Studded Parties on Instagram." Consequence of Sound. March 23, 2020. https://consequenceofsound.net/2020/03/d-nice-club-quarantine-instagram-live-guest-list/.

Schloss, Joseph G. *Making Beats: The Art of Sample-Based Hip-Hop*. Middletown: Wesleyan University Press, 2014.

Skeme Richards. "DJ Skeme Richards, the official DJ of the Red Bull BC One 2022 World Final." Technics. December 3, 2022. https://www.facebook.com/technics.global/videos/dj-skeme-richards-the-official-dj-of- the-red-bull-bc-one-2022-world-final/5008216262615440/.

Stoever, Jennifer Lynn. "Crate Digging Begins at Home: Black and Latinx Women Collecting and Selecting Records in the 1960s and 1970s Bronx." In *The Oxford Handbook of Hip Hop Music*. Edited by Justin D. Burton and Jason Lee Oakes, 1-21. Oxford: Oxford University Press, 2018.

Tatum, Alfred W. *Reading for their life:(Re) building the Textual Lineages of African American Adolescent Males*. Portsmouth: Heinemann, 2009.

Technics [https://www.facebook.com/technics.global/]. "DJ Skeme Richards, the official DJ of he Red Bull BC One 2022 World Final, has over 40 years of music and DJ experience. Let's find out what this legendary artist has to say about his passion, DJing! #technics #rediscovermusic #redbull #redbullbcone #breaking #sl1200 #vinyl #turntable." *Facebook*. 23 December 2022. https://www.facebook.com/technics.global/videos/5008216262615440.

Weheliye, Alexander. *Phonographies: Grooves in the Sonic Afro-Modernity*. Durham: Duke University Press, 2005.

Young, Vershawn Ashanti, and Michelle Bachelor Robinson, eds. *The Routledge Reader of African American Rhetoric: The Longue Durée of Black Voices*. New York: Routledge, 2018.

Yuna. "Broke Her." YouTube, December 3, 2014, video, 3:29, https://www.youtube.com/watch?v=XE9N8t7y4Dw.

Author Bio

Dr. Todd Craig is a professional professor at this rap science (Prodigy), who serves as the Marks Family Senior Director of the Marks Family Center for Excellence in Writing at the University of Pennsylvania. He teaches courses in Hip Hop Studies, Writing and Rhetoric, Urban Education and African American Studies.

Listening to Black Girls: Community Engaged Considerations of Intellectual Humility

Khirsten L. Scott, Elise Silva, Ariana Brazier

Abstract

This article explores the origins and evolution of HYPE Media, a youth-led media program grounded in Black feminist pedagogy, community listening, and intellectual humility. Through conceptual analysis, reflective narrative, and practical application, the authors examine how co-creation, vulnerability, and dialogic engagement shape ethical community-based research. By centering Black girls' voices, the work offers a model for transformative programming that challenges institutional norms and reimagines education as a practice of care, presence, and liberation.

Keywords: Black feminist pedagogy; intellectual humility; community listening; youth engagement; community engaged research; critical literacies; Black girlhood

One of the girls leaned back in her chair, the kind of lean that signals comfort, trust, and maybe even a little relief. "It's better this way," she said, glancing around the circle. "Now we can talk about the stuff we really care about." It was early 2020, and what had begun as a general youth media program had quietly transformed. The boys hadn't returned after winter break, not out of protest, just drift. What remained was a circle of Black girls, a handful of facilitators, and the beginnings of something sacred. That day, without fanfare or planning, the direction of HYPE Media shifted. The shift wasn't strategic or pre-planned. It was a response. Listening. A moment of clarity born from sitting with what was present, rather than forcing what was supposed to be.

This article is a story about dialogue, listening, and intellectual humility. It is a story about HYPE Media, Homewood Youth-Powered and Engaged Media, a project that began as a university-community partnership and evolved into a living exploration of Black feminist pedagogy. It was a space shaped by listening, built through co-creation, and sustained by the intellectual humility of those willing to learn with and from Black girls as they explored media, storytelling, and digital literacies as tools for self-definition, critique, and joy.

This article is conceptual, reflective, and practical all in one. Through it, we introduce you to the origin story of HYPE Media, focusing on its beginnings and evolution throughout the project's nascent years. As a conceptual piece, we make theoretical contributions by expanding and applying the theories of community listening and Black feminist practice to the idea of intellectual humility as a unique and novel way to approach community-engaged work. As a reflective piece, we show, through our own words and experiences, how community-engaged work is an act of simultaneous *doing* and *learning*—that the work informs the work, and that it is in the listening and deeply responsive moments of reflection and humility that a project's essence truly takes shape. In this sense, our reflections are demonstrations of inner dialogues and reflective learning on our part as authors, researchers, facilitators, and participants. Finally, it's practical in the explications of activities that we found to be meaningful applications of the concepts and theories we describe.

The practical moments come into focus as we reflect on specific play-based activities that shaped the early weeks of HYPE Media. These moments, though simple on the surface, embody the core concepts we explore throughout this piece: community listening and intellectual humility. Two games in particular, *The Question Game* and *Look Up, Look Down*, function as microcosms of our larger commitments. *The Question Game*, introduced in our very first session, served not only as the first activity but as a call to curiosity, vulnerability, and co-authorship. *Look Up, Look Down*, introduced later, deepened our collective capacity for presence, attentiveness, and relinquishing control. Together, these activities illustrate the power of engaging in open dialogue, embracing uncertainty, and recognizing the shared human experience of struggle. The lessons learned through these games extended far beyond the sessions in which they were played; they were conceptual anchors for our reflections and shaped how we understand the "ethics and practice of community engagement.

Throughout this piece, we argue that intellectual humility is a crucial component of community-based research and co-created programming. It demands that we recognize the complexity and iterative nature of the work, that we resist premature certainty, and that we remain open to being shaped by those we seek to learn with. For us, it also means acknowledging that our institutional affiliations must remain porous, accountable, and responsive. We show how this disposition fosters environments where mutual respect, shared value, and collaborative transformation are not just ideals, but daily practices

While you read, you'll encounter three voices, interwoven: Khirsten, a Black woman community educator, University of Pittsburgh professor, and founding facilitator of HYPE Media whose layers of literacy sponsorship (Brandt) shaped the project; Elise, a White woman trained in library and information science whose critical pedagogical approach invited us to see information as both method and intervention; and Ari, a queer Black woman organizer who grounded the program in a play-driven, abolitionist pedagogy who treats play as a serious and transformative way of knowing. We reflect at different moments in the piece about our involvement in HYPE Media and what we learned about community engagement, community listening, and intellectual humility throughout the process. Though we didn't set out with these theories in mind, they became clear to us through time and reflection as meaningful ways we were enacting the community-engaged work of HYPE Media. Our voices appear as vignettes that can be read alongside the theoretical and conceptual contributions at the beginning of the piece and the more practical overview of specific moments of community-engaged programming near the end of the piece.

An Introduction to HYPE Media

When we talk about the origins and evolution of HYPE Media, we must begin with place. HYPE didn't emerge in isolation, and it certainly wasn't the only thing happening. It grew out of a neighborhood already rich with commitment. Streets and homes filled with generations of neighbors and educators and artists and organizers and leaders who have long been doing the work of loving Black children, pushing back against systemic neglect, and building futures from what's been left behind. Homewood, Pittsburgh is one of those places. And while we name some of the partnerships that shaped HYPE's early days like Homewood Children's Village and the University of Pittsburgh's Community Engagement Center, we're careful not to center institutions. Instead, we center the energy of collaboration, the ethic of showing up, the slow trust-building, and the everyday practices of listening that made this work possible.

We were invited in, and we learned quickly that presence mattered more than plans. These early collaborations gave us the chance to listen deeply, to be shaped by the desires and dreams of Homewood youth, and to build a program that didn't just respond to a syllabus or a semester schedule, but to the rhythms of the community itself. Those rhythms were not always neat or predictable, but they were honest, teaching us what it means to practice educational justice from the ground up.

In cities like Pittsburgh, neighborhoods such as Homewood have long borne the consequences of systemic neglect, with policy decisions contributing to under-resourced schools, inconsistent youth programming, and a scarcity of opportunities for meaningful engagement (Pittsburgh Gender Equity Commission; Public Source). These patterns of disinvestment are not incidental; they reflect a broader national trend that disproportionately impacts Black communities and limits the educational and developmental infrastructure available to Black youth. But that's not the only story. The other story is the one we witnessed: the abundance of care, creativity, and possibility that emerges when people come together not to fix a place, but to be in relationship with it.

HYPE Media (Homewood Youth-Powered and Engaged Media) was born in 2019 from this spirit. It started as a collaboration between a University of Pittsburgh graduate seminar on Critical Literacies and Pedagogies, a course that aimed to move theory into practice by building with and learning from local youth, and Homewood Children's Village, a community-based organization in Pittsburgh dedicated to supporting the academic, social, and emotional development of children and families through cradle-to-career programming, partnerships, and place-based advocacy (Homewood Children's Village). Around the same time, the University of Pittsburgh opened its Community Engagement Center in Homewood, creating space for partnerships to develop across the Homewood neighborhood with the university (University of Pittsburgh). That timing was real. But the transformation didn't come from timing alone. Instead, it came from showing up, again and again. What began as a course assignment evolved into something more alive: a practice of listening, of witnessing, and of co-creating spaces where Black girls could speak freely, play loudly, and tell the stories they weren't often invited to tell.

The program was not simply a product of university outreach. It emerged from the intersecting needs for community-rooted learning, critical literacy development, and spaces where Black youth, particularly Black girls, could engage media on their own terms. At its core, HYPE Media was created to explore a question that has since guided every aspect of its work: What happens when we truly listen to Black girls?

Rooted in Pace, Guided by Presence

This guiding question was not rhetorical. It emerged in response to the layered and ongoing systemic inequities that Black girls face both locally and nationally—inequities grounded in racism, sexism, and the persistent societal failure to take their experiences seriously (Crenshaw, Ocen, & Nanda; Morris). Across the United States, and in Pittsburgh specifically, these realities are compounded by histories of disinvestment in Black neighborhoods like Homewood. Black girls in these spaces encounter the compounded harms of *misogynoir*, a term coined by Dr. Moya Bailey to describe the specific intersection of racism and sexism faced by Black women and girls (Bailey, 2010). These harms manifest as disproportionate disciplinary action (Morris, 2016), underrepresentation in enrichment programs like STEM and gifted education (Scott & White), and erasure from youth development initiatives.

HYPE Media was created as an intentional interruption of these patterns and rooted in the love, strategy, and the recognition that Black girls deserve spaces that nurture their creativity, leadership, and freedom. Although the program was initially open to all youth, it organically shifted its focus in early 2020 when only girls returned for the spring session. From that point forward, HYPE Media became a space not only for media creation but also for identity exploration, critical literacy, and empowerment through storytelling. The program embraced Black feminism as its method, theory, and ethic (Morris, 2019), grounding itself in lived experience, intersectionality, and co-construction as the foundation of its pedagogy and purpose.

HYPE Media's origin story, and this article, are deeply intertwined with the broader question of what it means to engage dialogically with communities, particularly through the lens of Black feminism and critical engagement with whiteness. Whiteness, as both an ideology and a structural system, perpetuates practices that marginalize Black girls by centering dominant cultural norms, erasing their voices, and rendering their experiences invisible in education and community programming (Crenshaw et al.; National Women's Law Center). These practices manifest in punitive educational systems (Morris, 2016) and societal narratives that pathologize or overburden Black girls with stereotypes of resilience, strength, or defiance (Bailey, 2010; Girls for Gender Equity).

By grounding HYPE Media in Black feminism and reflexivity, we demonstrate how theory and praxis can work together to disrupt these dynamics and foster transformative growth within community settings. The program intentionally centers the voices and experiences of Black girls, providing a space to counteract the erasures and exclusions upheld by whiteness. Intellectual humility emerges as a central method in this exploration, encouraging a shift from imposing solutions to co-creating spaces of liberation and possibility. Through HYPE Media, we engage dialogically to challenge and dismantle the systemic practices of whiteness, building pathways for more equitable, inclusive, and resonant community programs.

Tracing the Roots: A Founder's Narrative from Khirsten L. Scott

The origin story of HYPE Media is deeply tied to my own journey. This is not because the program reflects me, but because it grew out of the questions I was carrying and that were shaped by experience, dissonance, and hope. Before it became a project, HYPE was a longing.

In the fall of 2018, I moved to Pittsburgh to begin a tenure-track position in Composition and Rhetoric. I was the first Black woman in that role in my department. On paper, it was a milestone. But underneath, I was still searching for rootedness, for intellectual and cultural alignment, for a community that could hold me with both care and accountability as I navigated the layered pressures of academic life. I was looking for more than a position; I was looking for place.

That search began, quite literally, with trying to live. I needed to know where to get my hair braided, where to worship, where to find food that felt like home. One day, while visiting a local coffee shop in Homewood, I met a young Black girl who offered to help me find someone to braid my hair. She didn't just give me a recommendation; she offered me an entry point into conversation. And when I came back, she was there again. Our relationship unfolded slowly, through casual visits and small talk that grew into something more. It was a connection built not through programming or planning, but through noticing and returning.

In one of those conversations, I asked her what she liked to do in the neighborhood. Without hesitation, she told me, "There's nothing for me here." I was puzzled. There was a YMCA nearby. There were community sports. After-school programs. But she clarified, "There's nothing for *me*—for Black girls." That moment stopped me. She wasn't talking about availability. She was talking about belonging. I didn't have the language for it then, but that conversation became integral to my teaching of community listening as a practice as I navigated Pitt and Pittsburgh. She helped me understand that listening isn't just about hearing what's said: it can also be about honoring what's missing, what's felt, what's needed, and what's been repeatedly overlooked.

That same year, the University of Pittsburgh opened its Community Engagement Center in Homewood with intentions to foster university-community partnerships. I found myself drawn there, not because I had a plan, but because I had questions. What does it mean to engage ethically? What does it mean to be present without taking up too much space? What kind of engagement does a community like Homewood actually want?

I didn't find immediate answers. But I did find people—neighbors, organizers, youth workers—who were already asking their own questions, doing the work, and holding the complexity. It was in that in-between space, between my own longing and the ongoing work of others, that the early seeds of HYPE Media were planted. Not in isolation. Not in response to a grant or a syllabus. But through the accumulation of small moments: hair braiding suggestions, shared coffeeshop conversations, invitations to return, and the slow, sometimes uneasy, process of building trust.

Partnerships and Place-Making

My questions sharpened when I met Dr. John M. Wallace, Jr., a senior faculty member and endowed chair in the School of Social Work whose long-term presence in Pittsburgh's Homewood neighborhood created pathways for connection. Through him, I was introduced to his colleague Dr. Jamie Booth and, eventually, to Homewood Children's Village, a nonprofit deeply engaged in youth development and community-based work. These introductions didn't chart a path, but they offered me one layer of instruction as I began to find my way as a new professor attempting to do community-engaged work with care, humility, and responsiveness. Wallace added another layer of literacy sponsorship, bridging connections and offering financial support for early programming through the School of Social Work.

As the partnership developed, Homewood Children's Village became the primary community partner, following the Community Engagement Center's model of connecting university projects with neighborhood-based collaborators. Dr. Booth served as a faculty partner whose research and programming focused on overlapping youth populations, particularly around questions of safety and spatial justice. We didn't enter the work with identical projects or priorities, but we found shared ground through dialogue about youth work, about responsibility, and about what it means to design something with, rather than for, a community.

Following those initial introductions, we held several meetings where we discussed our respective projects, timelines, and values. There was no rush to define the work. Instead, we spent time learning about one another's commitments, sharing possibilities, and identifying needs from both sides. These early conversations became a kind of groundwork. Before anything was solidified—before there was a name, a plan, or a formal partnership—we were already practicing the kind of listening and reflection that would come to define HYPE Media. Eventually, we agreed to align the emerging collaboration with my graduate seminar, allowing the seminar and the program to grow alongside one another, each informing the other in real time.

At the time, I was preparing to teach a graduate seminar on Critical Literacies and Pedagogies. My background in writing studies, literacy theory, and digital culture provided a point of connection to questions already circulating in the Homewood community. I saw the course as an opportunity not just to teach theory, but to practice it and to build something responsive in collaboration with local youth, educators, and graduate students who were also longing for meaningful engagement.

But meaningful engagement required movement, literally and socially. I asked students to leave Oakland, to move beyond the university's core, and to pay attention to the journey. Each week, I encouraged them to take a different route to our seminar site in Homewood, whether by bus, carpool, bike, or walking, and to observe what they noticed internally, externally, and contextually. This wasn't just about getting from one place to another. It was about cultivating presence. We set aside time before and after each session for discussion and sensemaking. Those reflections became part of the learning. They helped set the tone for the kind of community-engaged work we were trying to do, which was work grounded in observation, reflection, and critical attunement to place.

The seminar eventually gave rise to what would become HYPE Media, which was then emerging to be a co-designed youth program that extended far beyond the seminar's curricular goals. But from the beginning, the work was not about placing a course in the community. It was about disrupting the assumed boundaries between university and neighborhood, theory and practice, research and relationship. It was about imagining what it means to approach literacy not only as skill, but as a method of liberation. The program offered a way of reading, naming, critiquing, and remaking the world.

Co-Theorizing Curriculum and Community

That vision shaped every design decision. I invited graduate students into the process not as assistants, but as co-designers. We centered storytelling as a method of learning and resistance. We built lesson plans around what the girls brought into the room—music, language, memories, silence, critique. We listened. We adapted. We stayed with the questions. And in doing so, we allowed the curriculum to emerge not from institutional expectation, but from what felt real, necessary, and alive.

While I had the deep honor of working alongside Black women who knew firsthand the demands and violences of the academy, I was also aware of the institutional realities. Black women remain statistically underrepresented in doctoral programs at Pitt and nationally (NCES; The Journal of Blacks in Higher Education). As a result, the graduate students who joined HYPE brought a range of racial identities, disciplinary trainings, and life experiences. What united them was a curiosity about what community-engaged learning could look like beyond the university, and a desire to move with integrity between theory and practice. Together, we established something that could hold that complexity, a space where we could learn by listening, build by co-creating, and show up not with answers but with a willingness to be changed.

Some of the graduate students had worked in neighborhood and educational spaces long before pursuing doctoral study; others were still learning how to navigate the ethical tensions of partnership and presence. I created room for all of them to lead. This meant taking their questions seriously, honoring their prior knowledge, and inviting them to design the program *with* me and *with* the youth—not for them.

During that first semester, all of the enrolled students participated in shaping the early weeks of the program. There was never an expectation that they continue after the course ended, but several chose to stay and deepen their roles and relationships as the work evolved. One of those students was Ari Brazier, my doctoral advisee, who hadn't initially been enrolled in the seminar but joined us as the project was taking shape. Ari, a queer Black woman organizer and scholar, brought an expansive, play-first, play-driven, play-everything philosophy that transformed how we understood both curriculum and community. She challenged us to treat play not as an accessory or a strategy to reach youth, but as a central mode of knowing. Through her leadership, we explored how much we learn about ourselves, each other, the world, and the future through play. Her abolitionist commitments and collaborative methodologies pushed us to unlearn many of our assumptions about structure, authority, and linear progress.

Elise Silva, a White woman with a background in library and information science and a deep investment in critical pedagogy, offered a different but equally generative perspective. She helped us recognize the role of information, not as an afterthought but as a rich site for analysis, emotional processing, and grounding. Elise invited us to see information as both method and intervention, and to ask how we, as facilitators and participants, take in, circulate, question, and make meaning from the world around us. Her contributions challenged us to slow down, observe more closely, and articulate what was happening in real time (Silva and Scott).

Though Ari and Elise entered the work at different moments, they helped build HYPE Media's intellectual and cultural infrastructure. Their contributions were foundational. Together, we cultivated a dynamic learning environment grounded in joy, rigor, and accountability, while committing to shared values: equity, imagination, and co-creation.

I saw this as part of a broader commitment to mentorship as community-building. The graduate students were not present to study the community. They were part of it. We practiced reflexivity together. We wrote fieldnotes together. We processed missteps and celebrated insights together. We honored the intellectual labor of the youth and of one another. In doing so, we blurred the lines between teacher and learner, between facilitator and participant. We became co-theorists of a space that remained in motion.

This is how HYPE Media came to be, not simply as a program but as a methodology. It did not begin as a project to be implemented, but as a question to be lived. That question, and the listening practice it demands, shape the direction of this article.

To fully understand the theoretical and methodological foundations of HYPE Media, it is important to place this work within the broader scholarly landscape that informed its development. In the following section, we engage literature across Black girlhood studies, Black feminist thought, critical literacies, and community-engaged research. These frameworks provided grounding for our design choices and our critiques of dominant paradigms. They also clarify why HYPE Media is not merely an intervention. It is a refusal, a refusal of extractive research practices, of deficit narratives, and of disengaged institutional approaches to community work. Instead, HYPE Media offers a model of co-created, critically informed, justice-oriented engagement that places Black girls not on the margins of research and programming, but firmly at its center.

Review of Literature: The Landscape of Community Listening

Scholarship

In their foundational work on community writing and community listening, Fishman and Rosenberg call for more scholarship "modeling the complex, messy work of authentic engagement with community writing" (5). They emphasize that community listening must consider power dynamics, positionality, and the collaborative creation of meaningful partnerships. This approach moves beyond passive hearing to active, intentional engagement—engagement that involves communities in shaping research agendas and fosters spaces where individuals feel valued, heard, and empowered. Their work serves as a critical entry point for this discussion, particularly as it intersects with our methodological intervention on community listening and intellectual humility.

Yet such "messy" experiences allow for community-engaged programs to be rooted within lived experiences, and allow for all participants, researchers, facilitators, and partners to come together as first and foremost as people, with a willingness to share their own complicated experiences alongside each other (Boyett 30; Love). Given this disposition's underlying framework of Black feminist thought, intellectual humility, co-creation as praxis, and focus on active engagement, community listening is a central, ethical principle in community research and community-engaged programming. As Fishman and Rosenburg suggest, "Community listening arises from the recognition that none of us is ever outside of our communities. We are never teaching or researching or organizingor writing unmoored from the communities to which we belong, from what surrounds us, or from the people with whom we engage" (3). Black feminist thought values the interconnectedness of individuals within their communities and recognizes that meaningful, mutually beneficial research must arise from active, inclusive engagement with these communities. By acknowledging that researchers and participants are inextricably linked, learning with and from one another and their communities, HYPE Media works to center Black feminist principles of relationality and collective empowerment.

Black Feminist Thought as Methodological Intervention

Extending the call to remain grounded in the communities where we teach and learn, we position community listening as a praxis shaped and deepened by Black feminist thought. This orientation challenges extractive forms of engagement by centering the lived experiences of Black women and girls as sites of knowledge, theory, and political urgency. The concept of the "outsider within" offers a lens for understanding how Black girls navigate institutions that rely on their participation while denying their full humanity and insight (Collins, 1986). The framework of intersectionality helps clarify how overlapping systems of race, gender, class, and other social forces structure these experiences in ways that make Black girls both hypervisible through surveillance and invisible within dominant research paradigms (Crenshaw). In educational and institutional spaces, this often translates into being constantly monitored, disciplined, or framed as problems, while their perspectives, capacities, and leadership are ignored or devalued.

bell hooks extends this critique by emphasizing that teaching and research must be rooted in love, care, and healing. In *Teaching to Transgress*, she reframes pedagogy as a deeply relational and political act, one that creates the conditions for liberation rather than control (hooks). A Black feminist approach to community listening takes up this challenge by refusing neutrality or detachment. Instead, it commits to connection, responsibility, and the collective imagining of new possibilities. Listening, through this lens, is not just a method but a transformative act that affirms presence, cultivates trust, and creates space for shared meaning and justice.

By introducing these principles into the framework of community listening, we expand its ethical and methodological dimensions. Black feminist thought emphasizes relationality, collective empowerment, embodied knowledge, and a refusal of epistemic violence. These principles demand a transformation of the terms under which listening and engagement occur. In our work, listening begins with Black girls' lived experiences and unfolds through a recognition of their critical insight, refusal, and imagination as forms of theory. By starting with listening, those creating community programming whether research based, project based, or educationally based, can begin with a shared understanding upon which to build meaningful partnerships. Jennifer Bay considers such an approach as a focus on "immediate human needs" which may be different from what scholarly apparatuses or educational frameworks might assume when approaching a community partnership. In this sense, community listening requires an ability to approach communities with more nebulous objectives that will be shaped alongside communities as an ad hoc process. Such a willingness to iterate, change plans, and revise can be difficult to fit into linear, scientific-methods based, objective-driven research agendas often purported by universities.

In doing so, we embrace writing as a Black feminist research method, "a route to intimacy" through which Black women and girls reclaim voice, knowledge, and connection (Ohito & Loury). This form of writing does not just document experience; it practices intimacy, disrupts erasure, and centers purposefully Black-centered epistemologies. For HYPE Media, storytelling, journaling, and multimodal composition were not only tools for expression but acts of relational knowing, healing, and co-theorizing.

Building on this understanding of writing as an intimate, embodied practice, community listening emerges as a complementary feminist method that deepens the possibilities of relational research. Royster (1996), in "When the First Voice You Hear Is Not Your Own," reflects on the ethical tensions that surface when researchers engage across lines of difference. She emphasizes the need for humility, reflexivity, and rhetorical patience, particularly when the researcher is not the cultural or experiential insider. Her work urges scholars to attend closely to power, positionality, and the histories that shape interactions with communities. Ratcliffe (2005), through her concept of rhetorical listening, extends this commitment by offering a specific methodology for engaging across difference. Rather than listening to respond or to affirm one's own position, rhetorical listening calls for a sustained openness to others' frameworks and logics, especially those shaped by race, gender, and culture. Taken together, these approaches reinforce the importance of listening as a feminist and ethical practice. They insist that researchers resist assumptions, remain attentive to complexity, and recognize the multiple identities and roles that both they and their community partners bring to the research encounter.

While Royster and Ratcliffe helped us think critically about our own positions and the ethics of cross-cultural engagement, our work with HYPE also required us to turn our attention more fully toward the community itself, particularly the Black girls at the heart of the project. To do this, we drew on Black feminist contributions within writing studies that confront dominant, white-centered models of literacy and affirm Black feminist–womanist storytelling as a method of liberation, self-definition, and collective transformation (Kynard; Baker-Bell). Framed as "the practice of a Black Feminist imaginative," Black feminist pedagogy pushes beyond traditional classroom hierarchies, demanding that pedagogy itself be rewritten through the lived experiences, histories, and epistemologies of Black women (Kynard). This reimagining extends to language as well, where the false neutrality of "Standard English" is unmasked as a tool of white linguistic hegemony. An antiracist Black language pedagogy affirms Black English as both legitimate and powerful, positioning language as a central site of resistance and radical possibility (Baker-Bell). In this view, literacy is not a means of assimilation but a pathway toward justice, freedom, and collective transformation.

Listening in Practice

This work is further shaped by Black feminist approaches to community engagement and abolitionist pedagogy, which move beyond reformist impulses that frame communities or students as problems to be solved. Rather than focusing on correction or control, these approaches center practices grounded in local knowledge, collective joy, and self-determination (Caisey; Graham; Love). In this framing, communities are not seen as lacking but as already holding the tools, insights, and histories necessary for their own flourishing. Supporting this kind of community knowledge requires more than presence; it requires listening that is both intentional and critically informed. This is especially important when engaging with Black girls, whose daily lives are shaped by the overlapping forces of racism and sexism. Moya Bailey's concept of misogynoir helps name this specific form of oppression and invites a deeper understanding of the stakes involved. When Black girls offer critiques of school, society, or even our well-intentioned efforts, those critiques must not be treated as peripheral. Instead, they must be understood as essential to any ethical and transformative approach to research and program design (Bailey, 2021).

The ideological and structural forces of whiteness continue to shape the daily realities of Black girls, often rendering them invisible while simultaneously subjecting them to heightened surveillance and scrutiny. This paradox of hypervisibility has been theorized as a mechanism through which Black girls are seen only through stereotype, threat, or deviance, yet rarely recognized in their full humanity, complexity, or agency (Newton; Mowatt, French, & Malebranche; Wade). What emerges is a pattern of being constantly watched but rarely witnessed, constantly disciplined but seldom understood. These conditions echo longstanding critiques of controlling images, which function to distort and limit the ways Black girls are perceived and engaged (Collins).

In schools, this paradox is not abstract. It shows up in the disproportionate punishment of Black girls, the erasure of their histories and contributions from curricula, and the absence of environments that nurture their brilliance and creativity. Within this context, community listening, when rooted in Black feminist theory and writing-based practice, offers a deliberate challenge to these dynamics. It is a method of refusal that resists imposed narratives, a mode of reconstruction that centers lived experience, and a form of relational presence that values connection over control. By holding space for the truths Black girls carry, this listening reclaims the right to be heard on their own terms.

Examples from community literacy work further underscore the urgency and possibility of this approach. Storytelling has been shown to cultivate empathy and relational understanding across lines of difference (Stone). Practices such as "preparatory community listening" make visible the wealth of knowledge that communities hold, often before researchers or institutions are ready to recognize it (Rowan & Cavarallo). Acts of self-disclosure and vulnerability, when ethically engaged, can serve as bridges between participants and facilitators, opening space for deeper connection and insight (Lohr & Lindenman). In each case, the work of reclaiming voice—particularly for those historically excluded—emerges as central to ethical community engagement. While our approach builds on these foundations, the integration of Black feminist writing methods shifts the focus toward intimacy, collaborative theory-making, and shared meaning-making as core components of community listening.

Listening, in this sense, is not a neutral act. It is grounded in the understanding that none of us exists outside the influence or responsibilities of our communities. As Fishman and Rosenberg (2019) argue, we are always teaching, researching, and living in relation to the communities we belong to. Black feminist listening extends this insight by insisting that such relationality demands accountability. It asks not only what we hear, but how we hear, and with what consequence. This orientation transforms listening from a tool of information-gathering into a practice of mutual recognition and transformation.

Yet institutional contexts often fail to make these shifts. School districts and universities, particularly when engaging historically disenfranchised communities, continue to struggle with building authentic relationships and trust (Stanley & Gilzene). In response, listening must be more than strategic or performative. It must be restorative, grounded in humility, and oriented toward relationship-building rather than outcomes or optics. Only then can it contribute to the conditions necessary for justice-oriented collaboration and sustained change.

Intellectual Humility and Community Listening: A Perspective from Elise Silva

I was a member of the first cohort of graduate students who worked with HYPE Media as part of Dr. Khirsten L. Scott's graduate seminar Critical Literacies and Pedagogies Across Urban Education and Higher Education in 2019. The first half of the semester we engaged in readings about critical literacies and began to imagine what critical literacy community work might entail at large. The second half of the semester we moved to the university's Community Engagement Center (CEC); a university-operated building located in Homewood built for the purpose of community-engaged work. There, we co-created a community literacy program with participant involvement and input. We conceptualized it as both a program and a research project. My involvement was as a graduate student facilitator who was responsible for planning activities and executing them with my peers. I later acted as a facilitator and wrote on this program as part of my dissertation project.

As a white woman, and a PhD student, I felt the pull of various identities and power dynamics almost instantly when our in-person programming started. I felt the uncertainty of my student status, wondering where my "expertise" fit in such a space as a "researcher in training," especially in relation to Dr. Scott and other community leaders. Further, as someone who grew up in white suburbs and who had attended majority white institutions, I was acutely aware of the privilege of my embodiment. I was also a single mother, having returned later in life to complete a PhD affording me more life experience than some of my peers. Even so, I often felt a sense of uncertainty regarding my racial privilege and even my age while interacting with the Westinghouse High School 6-12 students and found myself over-analyzing each interaction for fear of doing something "wrong."

Most often this looked like me hanging back, not knowing when or how to interact. I told myself I was "listening" or "making space," but in time I came to realize I was being avoidant. That avoidance wasn't an act of listening; it was a way to shield myself from discomfort and it eventually cost me connection. This was an important period of growth for me and self-realization. While my intentions were well-meaning, they did not ultimately serve the group. Instead, they served to protect me so I would not have to feel discomfort in my whiteness.

Such a posture, I quickly learned, was more of a hinderance than a productive, collaborative stance. For collaboration requires working *with* people, not avoiding them. It also assumed that there was a "right" and "wrong" way to proceed, ultimately arising from fear of failure. Eventually I came to understand through working alongside the community members, my peers, and the participants, that growth and learning cannot happen without failure and the humility that comes from such a disposition.

This change in perspective I learned to name; it was an exercise in *intellectual humility*. As a former academic librarian I was well-versed in information literacy pedagogy, having taught university students research skills for many years. I already understood intellectual humility as a posture assumed by a researcher that reframes the research path as messy, complex, and iterative, with multiple voices and perspectives, creating space for multiplicity, open-mindedness, curiosity, and critical questioning. What happened throughout my involvement in HYPE Media was that I realized that kind of frame could be applied to moments of community-driven programming and research as well. It could be an embodied reality—not just a cognitive one.

My understanding of this orientation was borrowed from "The Framework for Information Literacy" adopted in 2016 by the Association for College and Research Libraries. A central frame of research practice is fostering an understanding that *research is a form of inquiry*. As researchers mature, they realize their end goal is not to definitively answer a question, but rather, that research is a mode of iterative questioning, a method of engagement that embraces the unknown ("Framework"). Embracing the unknown and starting from an open attitude of thoughtful questioning became key as a program and curriculum builder, and later facilitator who engaged with HYPE media as part of my dissertation project.

Ultimately, the practice of intellectual humility became central to my growth and understanding of community listening practice in action. It provided a method and conceptual basis for what listening could look like in these kinds of spaces. It is also central to how I engaged with HYPE Media in my dissertation (Silva). As I worked to establish thoughtful research practices, I soon realized that I would need to be self-reflective in not only how I asked research questions and how I engaged with program participants, but also in how I would eventually disseminate research findings.

Embracing Intellectual Humility in Research: A Practice of Community Listening

Intellectual humility has a long history, with roots in philosophy, psychology, and education (Krumrei-Mancuso). Intellectual humility, a sister-concept to cultural humility (Hurley et al.)—is the awareness of one's personal knowledge limitations. Intellectual humility is a philosophical virtue for which psychologists eventually created robust framework and measurement tools (Porter et al.). This has heavily influenced the field of education in recent years in terms of pedagogy and practice, particularly in creating learning situations in which participants are comfortable making mistakes to learn (Brower). The concept has been less applied to community listening and learning practices than it has to measurable, formalized school environments, and remains a gap worth exploring.

When considering how intellectual humility, as a concept, overlaps with community listening practices, one must return to the researchers' orientation. A mindful researcher who is practicing intellectual humility, realizes that many problems and questions are open-ended. They understand that part of the ethical engagement with the research process is approaching and acknowledging the boundaries of their not-knowing. Such a stance requires a researcher thinker who is "open to being wrong and slow to be dismissive of information that challenges preconceptions" (Becker 191). This positionality leaves open the door to multiple directions for questions, and various interpretations of "findings."

Practicing Humility as a Commitment to Ethical Engagement

Given the work HYPE was doing at the intersections of race, class, gender, and education, cultivating sensitivity in the research process was not optional; it was foundational. The project demanded a participatory space where both researchers and participants could be present as full people. Graduate students found themselves reflecting on their own embodiments and lived experiences, choosing to "research" themselves in tandem with their fieldwork alongside youth. This self-reflexivity became a mode of accountability. Intellectual humility functioned as a key practice of community listening in this context, creating conditions where the voices, perspectives, and uncertainties of all involved could be honored. It invited researchers to acknowledge the limits of their own knowledge, to remain open to being challenged, and to shift in response to what the community surfaced. In an environment like HYPE Media, where transformation was part of the process, this kind of humility was both necessary and generative.

This orientation toward intellectual humility shares deep resonance with Black feminist research frameworks that position inquiry as a relational, dialogic, and iterative practice (Rankin). Within these frameworks, lived experience is not supplemental to theory but central to the knowledge-making process. Relationships are not instrumental to research outcomes; they are part of the epistemological structure itself. This perspective challenges extractive or linear models of research by insisting that knowledge emerges through sustained engagement, care, and co-authorship. Intellectual humility, in this light, is not simply an individual trait. It is a collective practice that holds researchers accountable to the communities. They engage with and affirm the value of shared meaning-making over authoritative claims.

Through this framework, the research practices at HYPE were not only guided by Black feminist theory but were also transformed by it. The project evolved through acts of listening, reflection, and response, where researchers remained attuned to their own position while actively co-constructing knowledge with youth. Intellectual humility was not a concession of authority, but a commitment to presence, learning, and the belief that knowledge is most powerful when it is created together.

This grounding is especially vital in contexts like HYPE Media, where intellectual humility operates not only as a personal disposition but as a structural and relational ethic. Within a Black feminist epistemological framework, humility is understood as a practice that embraces complexity, resists domination, and insists on shared authority (Rankin). It is shaped by an awareness of how power circulates through research relationships and institutional spaces. Drawing on intersectional analysis as framed by Collins and Bilge (2016), this perspective recognizes that ethical research requires a decentering of the researcher's voice and a willingness to listen with care, attentiveness, and accountability. Intellectual humility in this sense is not abstract. It is a concrete practice of acting in ways that affirm relationality, honor difference, and prioritize care over control.

Within HYPE Media, this translated into practices of co-creation, sustained critique, and shared reflection. We resisted quick fixes or one-size-fits-all solutions. Instead, we asked: What does it mean to honor the lived knowledge of Black girls? How do we build structures that allow their insights—not just their participation—to shape the work? In this way, intellectual humility was not ancillary to the program's design. It was central to its ethical foundation.

By acknowledging and valuing one's own embodiment in research, this practice aligns with pedagogies that emphasize the interconnectedness of personal and communal experience. Through this lens, humility is not a soft skill or personality trait but an ethical imperative, a daily practice of listening, adjusting, and staying accountable to the communities with whom we engage. Black feminist thought provided the framework for that practice and the language to describe what we already felt to be true: that justice-oriented research must be slow, relational, dialogic, and led by those most affected.

Humility and Iterative Research Design

Within academia at large, intellectual humility has become more salient as scholars have begun to question passed-down disciplinary knowledge, research practices, and scholarly traditions. Indeed, in the social sciences, "a large number of scientific findings have been disproven, or become more doubtful, in recent years. One high-profile effort to retest 100 psychological experiments found only 40 percent replicated with more rigorous methods" (Resnick). Such crises in disciplinary knowledge encourage researchers from all modes of scholarship to re-think their research methodologies and the assumptions that underline them. Impactful researchers ask questions repeatedly in the process of gaining understanding, and those engaging such an approach in the context of community listening must ask those questions and wait for answers from their community partners without pressuring them for an answer they think fits their research agenda. This method of research recognizes this process as never-ending, that questions always beget more questions. Unlike the rote and linear scientific method in which researchers hypothesize, experiment, analyze, and replicate, an active listening disposition in these research situations seek to break away from straightforward study to splitting off on unknown trajectories, being open to possibilities.

Such modes of inquiry are not meandering, but instead are mindful, present, and inquisitive. Like the play with which we engaged the youth of Homewood, the messiness of questioning also affords new avenues of meaning-making. This includes dialogue, community building, and increasingly complex question asking rendering deeper and more profound outcomes as a result. In other words, community listening, in tandem with intellectual humility, allows for alternate meanings and engagement. It allows for alternative data, findings, programs, and ultimately evolving answers to community concerns.

As a final note, we recognize design connects to Black feminist principles by emphasizing intellectual humility and community listening as central to rethinking research methods. These principles value iterative, non-linear approaches that prioritize community voices and experiences, aligning with the idea that impactful researchers must ask questions and patiently wait for community responses. This method respects the ongoing nature of inquiry, acknowledging that questions lead to more questions, and it values the multiplicity of perspectives and possibilities.

Playing with Questions and Playing with Uncertainty: A Perspective

with Ari Brazier

Grounded in Black feminist thought, the theoretical framework of community listening and intellectual humility shaped every aspect of our work in HYPE Media, from daily activities to long-term projects. We came to understand that how we approached the small and the large with equal care was essential to building trust and practicing listening as both method and relation. In this section, I reflect on two early activities, the *Question Game* and *Look Up, Look Down*, as examples of how Black feminist pedagogy and dialogic learning can live in simple, replicable acts of play. These games were not just openings; they were grounding practices that made room for vulnerability, reflection, and shared discovery.

Although I wasn't enrolled in the course that met weekly to design and facilitate the HYPE program, I was present each week as a co-facilitator and collaborator. I was also Dr. Scott's doctoral advisee, working under her guidance as I developed my dissertation on play, memory, and freedom in Thomasville, Georgia (Brazier, 2021). That research, along with my ongoing work with the Youth Undoing Institutional Racism (YUIR) initiative in Pittsburgh, had already shaped our years of dialogue around youth-led community transformation, the stakes of pedagogies of play, and the possibilities of Black feminist praxis in informal learning spaces.

So, when HYPE emerged, it felt like an extension of those conversations. I took the bus each week to the CEC and brought with me not only a willingness to help but also a sense of responsibility, creativity, and deep investment in what we were trying to build together.

I remember the first day clearly. Dr. Scott was in her office, overwhelmed by the logistics of pulling together a brand-new program. I offered to help, and together we created the first session's agenda. I polished it up and sent it out to the group, and that document became our template. We returned to this evolving tool, week after week, not as something rigid, but as something we could adapt and reshape. With each session, we set intentions, identified themes, and attached play as our primary pedagogical practice. I brought in games—ones I had used with youth in YUIR, ones I had observed or created through my own research—because I believed in their power to open space, to disrupt, and to connect (Brazier, 2025).

Looking back, I now understand that this work was shaped not only by theoretical alignment, but also by the relational proximity and feminist posture we shared. In another world, with more funding or more supportive infrastructure for community engaged scholarship, I might have been a graduate research assistant on the project. But in the often-underfunded landscape of humanities-based community work, and in the still-emerging understanding of what it means for faculty to structure radical research collaborations within institutions, our collaboration took shape through care, trust, and mutual regard.

Black Feminist Foundations of Play

From the very beginning of HYPE, play was not treated as a break from instruction but as a method and mode of knowing. Drawing on Black feminist frameworks that view embodiment, vulnerability, and relationality as essential to learning, we approached play as a practice of presence and connection. Rather than reinforcing hierarchy, it created opportunities to engage across difference. Showing up fully—emotionally, intellectually, and physically—became a central part of how we built community. That fullness did not require perfection or consistency; it made space for partiality, fluctuation, and the different ways each of us had the capacity to give. We understood ourselves as whole not because we were always complete, but because we were received in our many layers, and it was in our togetherness that this wholeness became possible.

This understanding was shaped by an engaged pedagogy grounded in care, mutual recognition, and freedom (hooks, 1994). In designing activities, we treated play as a relational practice that invited everyone in the room, including youth, graduate students, faculty, and community members, to enter a space where learning was co-created rather than delivered. Play became a structure for noticing, for building trust, and for moving beyond extractive educational routines toward something more reciprocal and affirming.

Our commitment to proximity and shared feeling was also informed by the concept of wake work, which urges us to remain present with the afterlives of slavery through care, relational witnessing, and refusal (Sharpe). In the HYPE classroom, this meant staying with the emotional truths that young people carried, including grief, frustration, longing, and joy, and honoring those realities not only through serious reflection but through practices that made space for lightness, laughter, and breath. Play became a form of presence work, a way of acknowledging pain while still making room for possibility.

Activities like the *Question Game* and *Look Up, Look Down* were intentionally designed to hold this complexity. These were not simply icebreakers or energizers. They were practices of what Gumbs (2020) describes as collaborative survival, where movement and laughter became tools for connection, resistance, and renewal. These games created space for Black girls to speak, to be witnessed, to lead, and to experience themselves outside the gaze of discipline or deficit. The space held by play affirmed that survival is not just about enduring but about breathing together, as Gumbs writes, and about creating new ways to care and be cared for.

This framework aligns with a healing-centered approach that views restoration as a collective process grounded in agency, cultural identity, and meaningful relationships (Ginwright). Within this context, play was not simply a strategy for engagement. It became a way of navigating reality without surveillance, a space where students and adults could imagine something freer. Healing, in this view, did not depend on correction or closure. It depended on return, on the practice of showing up, again and again, with curiosity, care, and openness to change.

Taken together, these frameworks challenge the idea that play is peripheral to learning. Instead, they reveal its pedagogical and methodological significance. The games we played opened portals into deeper relational work, inviting us to risk connection, to listen with our full selves, and to co-create meaning in the moment. These practices, grounded in Black feminist thought, were expressions of both survival and freedom. What emerged at HYPE was not simply a curriculum. It was a living practice shaped in real time with the girls. It was built through presence, attunement, and a kind of listening that exceeded language. Play, care, and collaborative survival were not additions to the program. They formed its very foundation.

The Question Game

Our first session began with *The Question Game*, a simple but powerful activity that laid the foundation for how we would engage with one another. With the room buzzing with uncertainty, excitement, and energy, we invited everyone (youth, graduate students, faculty, and community partners) to stand in a circle. Each person asked the person to their left a question, any question: What time is it? Why are you wearing shoes? Is it raining outside? What did you eat for lunch? How tall are you? And so on. Without responding, laughing, or hesitating, that person then turned to their left and asked a different question. Questions could not be repeated, and anyone who did, or who laughed or hesitated, was "out."

We started with this game to ensure everyone felt comfortable asking potentially uncomfortable, ridiculous, or difficult questions. It wasn't simply an icebreaker; it was an invitation into a different kind of intellectual and relational space. It aligned with our theoretical engagement with community listening, beginning with a vulnerable question to initiate dialogue. This seemingly light-hearted exercise challenged us to move beyond our comfort zones and embrace the discomfort and vulnerability of asking. In doing so, we intentionally disrupted traditional power dynamics often present in educational settings. Rather than assuming the role of experts, faculty and graduate students embraced uncertainty, acknowledging our shared journey of co-learning.

The act of asking, rather than answering, became a cornerstone of our collective interaction.

This dynamic served as a constant reminder that we were not there to deliver solutions or impose knowledge. Instead, we were committed to understanding, listening, and learning together which foregrounded the kind of intellectual humility that values curiosity over certainty. The game required us to question our assumptions about one another, particularly those shaped by geography, education, roles, social identities, and lived experiences. It reflected principles that value multiplicity, relationality, and the disruption of hierarchy, fostering a space where all voices were welcomed and all questions were worthy.

The game also exemplified a deeply rooted Black feminist ethic. It mirrored and extended Black feminist commitments to honoring situated knowledge, embracing dialogue, and resisting systems that marginalize through control, surveillance, or expertise. Together, we witnessed that knowledge is never universal but always situated, that every voice carries a history, and that recognizing standpoint is crucial to a fuller understanding of the world (Collins, 1990). The iterative nature of the questioning echoed bell hooks' call to teach from a place of continuous learning and unlearning.

In this sense, we were not only playing a game, we were modeling a practice of collective inquiry and community accountability.

This approach to learning was a living, breathing practice shaped in real time with the girls, rooted in presence, attunement, and listening beyond words. It reflected a pedagogy of being with rather than doing to—a relational practice that made space for joy, experimentation, and mutual care. Play, care, and collective survival were not add-ons to the program; they formed its very foundation. In hindsight, the Question Game marked our first shared experience of intellectual humility. It flipped classroom expectations by privileging the question over the answer, uncertainty over expertise. We invited play into our pedagogy and practiced what it meant to listen deeply and learn relationally.

Look Up, Look Down

In another early session, we introduced a game called *Look Up, Look Down*. Everyone stood in a circle with their heads bowed. On the cue "Look up," each person searched for someone else's gaze. If two people locked eyes, they screamed and exited the circle. Then came the next cue: "Look down." The rhythm repeated, drawing participants into a cycle of anticipation, connection, and awareness.

The scream wasn't in the original game—or at least, we don't think it was—but Ari added it. It became essential, creating a moment of silliness, but also intimacy. In HYPE, silliness was never seen as frivolous. It was a mode of learning, a rehearsal of trust. We understood that students are often conditioned out of intimacy in formal education. Eye contact is seen as threatening; laughter is seen as disruptive; and play is either infantilized or dismissed altogether. But for us, play was a serious method. *Look Up, Look Down* was a way of practicing being seen, of noticing what happens when eyes meet, even briefly, and of asking what it means to be present with and for one another.

Many students avoided eye contact altogether, and we noticed that not as defiance or disobedience, but as a kind of signal. It told us something about how often Black girls are observed, surveilled, or corrected, but rarely witnessed. That distinction mattered and this game created space to disrupt those dynamics. Rather than reinforcing a culture of compliance or control, it invited the girls to move toward each other on their own terms. In doing so, they practiced forms of relational presence that extended beyond the moment of the game.

The act of locking eyes, screaming, and stepping out of the circle became more than play; it became symbolic. It surfaced shared tensions and gestures of exposure, collision, and recovery. The youth were navigating complex realities in a rapidly gentrifying, historically Black neighborhood. While our experiences differed, this activity offered a moment of togetherness, a collective acknowledgment of what it means to be seen, startled, and still held. In these seemingly small actions, we were rehearsing radical healing.

The structure of the game demanded responsiveness. There was no winner, no expert, no endpoint, only participation. It reminded us that curriculum can be lived in the body, in breath, in the shared experience of movement and laughter. By leaning into the awkwardness and absurdity of the moment, we built a kind of lateral alignment. There was nothing to perform, no rubric to satisfy. Instead, we built a practice of collective presence and awareness, one that included ourselves, each other, and the possibilities we were creating together.

Look Up, Look Down reflected Black feminist commitments to embodiment, relationality, and care. It modeled what it means to learn through proximity and to recognize how deeply we are entangled in one another's lives. Each gesture—eye contact, scream, exit—held layers of meaning about protection, resistance, and tenderness. We were not just surviving these moments, we were shaping new ones, together.

This activity, like others in HYPE, demanded intellectual humility. It required our full presence and asked us to approach even a game with curiosity rather than control. We had to be willing to release our assumptions, lean into uncertainty, and let ourselves be changed by what emerged. These were not just moments of play; they were moments of pedagogy. And in HYPE, that pedagogy was always rooted in care, relationship, and the radical possibility of learning together.

Games like *The Question Game* and *Look Up, Look Down* were not diversions or add-ons. They were intentional, co-created practices that asked: What do students need? What can we build together? And how might we come to know, not through mastery, but through mutual presence? These games made our shared commitments to play, to listening, to witnessing, to humility visible. Together, they offered a model for learning that was as joyful as it was rigorous, as serious as it was liberating, and as rooted in Black feminist tradition as it was in the here and now.

Conclusion

We believe that HYPE Media offers a dynamic blueprint for fostering deep engagement, resisting systems of superficiality and whiteness in its approach. It demonstrates the power of dismantling systemic inequities and building futures rooted in dialogue, a commitment to unlearning, re-doing, failing, and embracing the messy, iterative nature of deep community collaboration. The program's impact is evident in the words of one participant, who years later, reflected on her memories of the Question Game as part of a program assessment interview: "And it's like, stuff [like that] that catches people off guard…That was my favorite [game] because of the unexpectedness; it made it funny. [Peoples'] personalities] made it fun." This reflection encapsulates the core principles of HYPE Media—that community building thrives in the unexpected, that asking questions opens people to new ways of thinking, and that joy and vulnerability dialogically and interconnectedly evolve together.

Reflecting on our journey with HYPE Media, we realize how deeply it transformed our understanding of community engagement and the principles of Black feminist thought. The emphasis on listening deeply, valuing diverse voices, and embracing the iterative nature of learning has reshaped our approach to both research and personal interactions. Witnessing the growth and empowerment of the Homewood youth, we saw firsthand the power of creating spaces where their voices are not only heard but central to shaping, leading, and living the conversation.

As three researchers from different positionalities, informed by our interaction with other researchers, students, and community participants, we offer these reflections to highlight the relational and community-centered nature of HYPE Media. Our diverse perspectives have enriched the program and the program has enriched us, demonstrating the value of collaborative approaches in addressing systemic issues. HYPE Media's contributions are essential to the fields of community engagement, literacy studies, and writing studies. This work underscores the importance of integrating Black feminist thought, community listening, and intellectual humility into academic and practical frameworks. By prioritizing the voices and experiences of marginalized communities, we challenge conventional methodologies and highlight the value of co-constructed knowledge. These principles encourage a shift from top-down approaches to ones that foster shared agency and mutual respect.

Incorporating the insights from Black feminist thought into community literacy and writing studies provides a richer, more inclusive understanding of these fields. The iterative, non-linear approaches emphasized by HYPE Media align with the dynamic and evolving nature of community engagement. Scholars and practitioners alike can learn from this model, recognizing that meaningful programming is built through collaborative, dialogic processes for the purposes of the community. Intellectual humility, as practiced in HYPE Media, reminds us that embracing uncertainty and vulnerability is crucial for transformative learning and growth. Ultimately, this work exemplifies how integrating these principles can lead to more effective and impactful community-engaged scholarship and practice.

Acknowledgments

With deep gratitude, we thank the Black girls—Amber, Tereisa, Ny'Ela, Vonda, Sanai, La'Niya, Nadia, Kamyiah, Dejahne, Kayla, Ny'Jay, Tati, Drea, Zoe, and Mir Mir—whose brilliance, courage, and creativity made this work not only possible, but meaningful. Thank you to the families and community members who trusted and supported this vision, and to the graduate students—CE Mackenzie, Taylor Waits, Nick Avery, Elise Silva, Nate Lattanzio, Sana Karim, Jess Batychenko, and Megan Donnelly—whose thinking, exploration, and writing helped shape the early foundations of this project. We extend sincere thanks to Dr. Jamie Booth, Dr. John M. Wallace, Jr, Dr. Daren Ellerbee, Dr. Lina Dostilio, and Dr. Keith Caldwell as well as the staff at the Community Engagement Center and the University of Pittsburgh's Office of Community Engagement, for their steadfast belief in the work. We are especially grateful to Homewood Children's Village—and in particular to JaLissa Coffee Lyon—for your unwavering support in building and sustaining this vision. To the staff, Public Allies, and AmeriCorps members who contributed to HCV's work: thank you for your care, energy, and commitment. May we all continue with love and thoughtful intention in this work.

Works Cited

"A City Divided: Pittsburgh's Inequality Across Race and Gender." PublicSource, 2019.

Bailey, Moya. "They Aren't Talking About Me…" Feminist Media Studies, vol. 10, no. 1, 2010, pp. 69–86.

—. *Misogynoir Transformed: Black Women's Digital Resistance*. New York University Press, 2021

Baker-Bell, April. *Linguistic Justice: Black Language, Literacy, Identity, and Pedagogy*. Routledge, 2020.

Bay, Jennifer L. "Research Justice as Reciprocity: Homegrown Research Methodologies." *Community Literacy Journal*, vol. 14, no. 1, 2019), pp. 7-25.

Becker, Bernd W. "The Librarian's Information War." *Behavioral & Social Sciences Librarian*, no. 35, vol. 4, 2016, pp.188-191. doi: 10.1080/01639269.2016.1284525

Boyett, Megen Farrow. *Acting on What We Hear: The Impact of a Listening Methodology in a Community Literacy Program*. 2021. University of Louisville, PhD Dissertation.

Brandt, Deborah. "Sponsors of Literacy." College Composition and Communication, vol. 49, no. 2, 1998, pp. 165-185.

Brazier, Ariana. *"Yea. I'm in my hood. No strap": Black Child Play as Praxis & Community Sustenance*. 2021. University of Pittsburgh, PhD Dissertation.

—. Imagination Playbook. 2025, www.imaginationplaybook.com/.

Brower, Emily. "How Classrooms Can Promote Intellectual Humility—Or Discourage It." 15 March, 2023. https://greatergood.berkeley.edu/article/item/how_classrooms_can_promote_intellectual_humility_or_discourage_it

Caisey, Alannah. *Black Women's Liberatory Pedagogies: Towards a Transformative Theory and Praxis*. 2023. University of Pittsburgh, PhD Dissertation.

Collins, Patricia Hill."Learning from the Outsider Within: The Sociological Significance of Black Feminist Thought." Social Problems, vol. 33, no. 6, 1986, pp. S14–S32.

—. *Black Feminist Thought: Knowledge, Consciousness, and the Politics of Empowerment*. Boston: Unwin Hyman, 1990.

Crenshaw, Kimberlé. "Mapping the Margins: Intersectionality, Identity Politics, and Violence against Women of Color." Stanford Law Review, vol. 43, no. 6, 1991, pp. 1241–1299.

Crenshaw, Kimberlé Williams, Priscilla Ocen, and Jyoti Nanda. Black Girls Matter: Pushed Out, Overpoliced and Underprotected. African American Policy Forum, 2015.

"Framework for Information Literacy for Higher Education." *Association of College and Research Libraries, a Division of the American Library Association*. 2016. https://www.ala.org/acrl/standards/ilframework

Fishman, Jenn, and Lauren Rosenberg. "Guest Editors' Introduction: Community Writing, Community Listening." *Community Literacy Journal*, vol. 13, no. 1, 2019, pp. 1-4. doi:10.25148/clj.13.1.009085.

Gender Equity Commission, City of Pittsburgh. Pittsburgh's Inequality Across Gender and Race. Sept. 2019.

Ginwright, Shawn A. *Black Youth Rising: Activism and Radical Healing in Urban America*. Teachers College Press, 2010.

Girls for Gender Equity. "Black Girls Matter: Creating Safe Spaces." Girls for Gender Equity, n.d., ggenyc.org.

Graham, DaVonna. *Always Black, Always Woman; An Examination of Black Feminist Activism in Education*. 2022. University of Pittsburgh, PhD Dissertation.

Gumbs, Alexis Pauline. *Dub: Finding Ceremony*. Duke University Press, 2020.

"Homewood Children's Village." Homewood Children's Village, 2025, hcvpgh.org.

hooks, bell. Teaching to Transgress: Education as the Practice of Freedom. Routledge, 1994.

Hurley, David A., et al. *Cultural Humility*. 1st ed., American Library Association, 2022.

Krumrei-Mancuso, Elizabeth J. "Intellectual Humility." *Open Encyclopedia of Cognitive Science*, 24 Jan. 2025, https://doi.org/10.21428/e2759450.f00bd0fc.

Kynard, Carmen. *Vernacular Insurrections: Race, Black Protest, and the New Century in Composition-Literacies Studies*. State University of New York Press, 2013.

Lohr, Justin, and Heather Lindenman. "Challenging Audiences to Listen: The Performance of Self-Disclosure in Community Writing Projects." *Community Literacy Journal*, vol. 13, no. 1, 2019, pp. 71-86. doi:10.25148/clj.13.1.009091.

Love, Bettina L. "A ratchet lens: Black queer youth, agency, hip hop, and the Black ratchet imagination." *Educational Researcher*, vol. 46, no. 9, 2017, 539-547.

Morris, Monique W. *Pushout: The Criminalization of Black Girls in Schools*. The New Press, 2016.

—. *Sing a Rhythm, Dance a Blues: Education for the Liberation of Black and Brown Girls*. The New Press, 2019.

Mowatt, Rasul A., Bryana H. French, and Dominique A. Malebranche. "Black/Female/Body Hypervisibility and Invisibility: A Black Feminist Augmentation of Feminist Leisure Research." Journal of Leisure Research, vol. 45, no. 5, 2013, pp. 644–660. National Recreation and Park Association.

National Center for Education Statistics. "Fast Facts: Degrees Conferred by Race/Ethnicity and Sex." nces.ed.gov, U.S. Department of Education, 2024, https://nces.ed.gov/fastfacts/display.asp?id=72.

National Women's Law Center. Let Her Learn: Stopping School Pushout for Girls of Color. 2017.

Newton, Veronica A. "Hypervisibility and Invisibility: Black Women's Experiences with Gendered Racial Microaggressions on a White Campus." Sociology of Race and Ethnicity, vol. 9, no. 2, 2023, pp. 164–178.

Ohito, Esther O., and Amirah Loury. "I Write With Intent: Writing as a Black Feminist Research Method and Route to Intimacy." Qualitative Inquiry, vol. 30, no. 7, 2024, pp. 595–608. https://doi.org/10.1177/10778004241269993.

Porter, Tenelle et al. "Predictors and Consequences of Intellectual Humility." *Nature Reviews Psychology* vol. 1,9 (2022): 524-536. doi:10.1038/s44159-022-00081-9

Rankin, Yolanda A. "Moving from Theory to Application: Black Feminist Thought as an Intersectional Framework for Design." ACM Interactions, Sept.–Oct. 2024.

Ratcliffe, Krista. *Rhetorical Listening: Identification, Gender, Whiteness.* Southern IL UP, 2005.

Resnick, Brian. "Intellectual Humility: The Importance of Knowing You Might Be Wrong." *Vox,* 4 Jan. 2019, https://www.vox.com/science-and-health/2019/1/4/17989224/intellectual-humility-explained-psychology-replication.

Rowan, Karen, and Alexandra Cavallaro. "Toward a Model for Preparatory Community Listening." *Community Literacy Journal,* vol. 13, no. 1, 2019, pp. 23-36. doi:10.25148/clj.13.1.009088.

Royster, Jacqueline Jones. "When the first Voice You Hear is Not Your Own." *College Composition & Communication,* vol. 47, no. 1, 1996, pp. 29-40.

Scott, Kimberly A., and M. White. "Compounding Inequity: The Intersection of Race and Gender in STEM Education." 2013.

Sharpe, Christina. *In the Wake: On Blackness and Being.* Duke University Press, 2016.

Silva, Elise. *Authority, Information Justice, and Source-Based Writing: Cultivating a Critically Curious Research Disposition.* 2023. University of Pittsburgh, PhD Dissertation.

Silva, Elise, and Khirsten Scott. "Developing Black Feminist Researcher Identities: A Youth-Engaged Wikipedia Case Study in Information Activism." *Journal of Information Literacy,* vol. 17, no. 1, 2023, https://journals.cilip.org.uk/jil/article/view/24. https://doi.org/10.11645/17.1.3359.

Stanley, Darrius A., and Alounso Gilzene. "Listening, Engaging, Advocating and Partnering (LEAP): A Model for Responsible Community Engagement for Educational Leaders." *Journal of Research on Leadership Education,* vol. 18, no. 2, 2023, pp. 253-276.

Stone, Erica M. "The Story of Sound Off: A Community Writing/ Community Listening Experiment." *Community Literacy Journal,* vol. 13, no. 1, 2019, pp. 16-22. doi:10.25148/clj.13.1.009087.

"The Number of African American Doctorates Reaches an All-Time High." The Journal of Blacks in Higher Education, 12 Dec. 2024, https://jbhe.com/2024/12/the-number-of-african-american-doctorates-reaches-an-all-time-high-2/.

University of Pittsburgh. "Community Engagement Center in Homewood." Community Engagement Center, 2025, www.cec.pitt.edu/homewood.

Wade, Ashleigh Greene. *Black Girl Autopoetics: Agency in Everyday Digital Practice.* Duke University Press, 2024.

Wallace, John M., Jr. "Withintrification™: Transforming A Community From The Inside Out." Bible Center Church Built Environment Report 1956–2024. Bible Center Church, Dec. 2024.

Wallace, John M., Jr., Valerie L. Myers, and Jim Holley. Holistic Faith-Based Development: Toward a Conceptual Framework. The Roundtable on Religion and Social Welfare Policy, Rockefeller Institute of Government, Apr. 2004.

Authors' Bios

Khirsten L. Scott, PhD is an Assistant Professor in the University of Pittsburgh's School of Education and Director of the Western Pennsylvania Writing Project. Her scholarship and community work center Black feminist and womanist practice across rhetorical theory, writing studies, digital and Black studies, and critical pedagogy. She leads HYPE Media, a youth-powered storytelling initiative in Pittsburgh, and co-founded DBLAC, a national network supporting Black scholars. Her work has appeared in *Kairos*, Composition Studies, *Prose Studies*, *The Routledge Reader of African American Rhetoric*, and other venues. Dr. Scott is the 2024 recipient of the Ernest A. Lynton Award for the Scholarship of Engagement from Campus Compact.

Elise Silva, PhD is the Director of Policy Research at Pitt Cyber, where she studies the intersections of technology, society, and public policy. Drawing on humanistic analysis, social science methods, and a community-engaged approach, her work has appeared in *Journal of Information Literacy*, *Tech Policy Press*, and other venues. She previously served as an academic librarian and visiting English faculty at Brigham Young University. Dr. Silva holds a PhD in Writing Studies from the University of Pittsburgh, an MLIS from the University of North Texas, and an MA in English from BYU. Her honors include an honorable mention for the 2024 *Computers and Composition* Hugh Burns Distinguished Dissertation Award, a 2022 Mellon Predoctoral Fellowship, a 2020 Sawyer Seminar Information Ecosystems Fellowship, and the 2017 ALA Library Instruction Round Table Innovation Award.

Ariana Brazier, PhD is a Black queer feminist and smiley sad mom-girl. She is a play-driven community organizer and educator who is motivated to raise a joyous, free Black child. Ari received her doctoral degree in English, Critical & Cultural Studies from the University of Pittsburgh in April 2021. She now resides in Atlanta, GA. Ari has been described by the people she loves as Southern, explosive, abstract, intricate, and awkward.

Feeling Like a Writer: Composing & Publishing Writer's Memos in a University-Adjacent Writing Group for Low-Income Adults

Gabrielle Isabel Kelenyi

Abstract

In this article, I describe a pedagogical practice that I argue can augment community publishing's potential to help adult undergraduate students' writerly confidence to help them *feel like writers* and build affirming relationships with wider audiences: writer's memos. Because writer's memos are opportunities for writers to demonstrate and build their rhetorical awareness and skills, they serve as mechanisms for building (and act as living representations of) one's writerly self-efficacy. However, other than *Community Literacy Journal*'s Coda Section, which asks for reflections to accompany the creative work it publishes, the use of writer's memos in community publishing for marginalized individuals has not been widely adopted or explored. Data from semi-structured interviews and collaborative field texts suggest that including writer's memos in community publishing efforts can have positive implications for writers themselves and reader-writer relationships in community writing. Writer's memos can help build meaningful and affirming relationships across difference between readers and writers: they can showcase how writers and readers can work together to revise socially constructed notions of who gets to read and be read, thereby enacting social change via community publishing.

Keywords: writer's memos, community publishing, writerly self-efficacy

Introduction

The editors of *Circulating Communities: The Tactics and Strategies of Community Publishing* describe community publishing as "the consistent effort to develop pedagogies and practices which allow marginalized individuals and groups to self-organize and gain a platform to speak publicly on their own terms to the larger community" (Mathieu, Parks, & Rousculp, 10). Relatedly, Laurie J. C. Cella and Jessica Restaino, editors of *Unsustainable: Re-Imagining Community Literacy, Public Writing, Service-Learning, and the University,* assert that students can come to "a deeper understanding of their local communities" through a community-engaged composition curriculum that emphasizes the exchange of ideas and information (3). Both edited collections frame community-engagement—in the form of community-university partnerships/projects for Cella and Restaino and community publishing for Mathieu et al.— as a *pedagogical practice* that builds skills, knowledges, and discourses for the community writers and/or student writers involved.

Community publishing has the potential to dismantle deficit perspectives that adult undergraduate writers themselves and others hold about their writerly identities (Perry et al.). According to Mathieu, Parks, and Rousculp, community publishing champions "community control over their own representations," which in turn allows it to help enact social change (Mathieu, et al. 10). The *Circulating Communities* editors explain how 'being in print' helps situate various people—such as academics, politicians, celebrities, etc.— as "'intellectuals,' or at least as demonstrating that their lives have a value to others" (Mathieu, et al. 2). For the population considered in this article, however, multiply-marginalized adult writers, the positioning of writers as "intellectuals" that Mathieu et al. attribute to 'being in print' isn't necessarily so easy due to this diverse group's complex relationships with writing and readers (Wells; Greenberg; Rosenberg). Nonetheless, it is important to help them strengthen their abilities to *feel like writers*. Feeling like a writer is a concept I adapted from literature on writerly self-efficacy that emphasizes connections between being successful at writing tasks and writerly development. While writerly self-efficacy literature often addresses K-16 contexts and does not take into account race and class, I find it useful for thinking about the potential of community publishing for multiply-marginalized adult undergraduate writers. Writing studies scholars know that writing (re)produces possibilities for inequity (Adler-Kassner & Wardle; Byrd). This is especially true for adult undergraduates, students who have taken alternative paths to and through higher education. Adult undergraduates have often been academically disenfranchised due to structural oppression and inequities such as colorblind racism, neoliberal disenfranchisement, and the literacy myth (Schrantz; Miller Brown; Lundberg et al.; Wells; Greenberg; Rosenberg; Graff). This exclusion negatively affects their writerly self-efficacy.[1] Community publishing's potential to help dismantle deficit perspectives on adult undergraduate writers' self-efficacy is likely because of "the resonant meaning of 'being in print' that carries importance for many individuals" (Mathieu, et al. 2). This helps being published gain a sense of prestige (Mathieu, et al. 2): as Sara Guest, Hanna Neuschwander, and Robyn Steely write about in "Respect, Writing, Community: Write Around Portland," "the chance to be published is a huge and lasting boost of self-esteem" (51).

In this article, I describe a pedagogical practice that I argue can augment community publishing's potential to help adult undergraduate students' writerly confidence, to help them *feel like writers* and build affirming relationships with wider audiences: writer's memos. Writer's memos (also referred to as process memos or reflective writing) have typically been used in composition classrooms to enhance student-instructor dialogue, reinforce and self-assess lessons learned and/or growth, as well as enhance metacognition, among other uses (Sommers; "The Writer's Memo"). In addition to helping writers become more effective readers and revisers of their own work, writer's memos also position readers "to adopt constructive roles as respondents" ("The Writer's Memo"). These functions of writer's memos are particularly important to community literacy projects and community publishing efforts because they can help amplify the boost to writers' self-esteem mentioned by Guest, Neuschwander, and Steely. That is, because writer's memos are opportunities for writers to demonstrate and build their rhetorical awareness and skills, they serve as mechanisms for building (not to mention, act as living representations of) one's writerly self-efficacy. And when community writers are confident in their own writing competence, they can be confident in how they represent themselves in their writing, helping them achieve their social change goals via their writing projects. However, other than *Community Literacy Journal*'s Coda Section, which asks for reflections to accompany the creative work it publishes, the use of writer's memos in community publishing for marginalized individuals has not, to my knowledge, been widely adopted or explored.

Here I offer a description of the impetus for and impacts of composing and publishing writer's memos alongside creative writing by members of a community writing group for adult undergraduate students called Our Writing Group (OWG).[2] This pedagogical practice not only helped the members of OWG build skills, knowledges, and discourses regarding writing but also stimulated their active and positive engagement with readers, thereby enhancing their abilities to *feel like writers*. In the sections that follow, I will provide more details about OWG and my research with the group and use data from semi-structured interviews with OWG writers to establish how group members' previous reader-writer relationships impacted their writerly identities. Then, I will use excerpts from writer's memos authored by participants and published in OWG's publication, *OWG Oracle*, to illustrate how this pedagogical practice can help amplify the positive effects community publishing can have on writerly self-efficacy. Overall, the results of this analysis indicate that including writer's memos in community publishing efforts can have positive implications for writers themselves and reader-writer relationships in community writing and that this pedagogical practice is useful beyond the composition classroom. Writer's memos can help build meaningful and affirming relationships across difference between readers and writers; thus, they belong in community publishing, especially for multiply-marginalized authors.

Community-University Context & Data Collection

Our Writing Group (OWG) is a community writing group for alumni of Venture, a humanities-based, university-sponsored program, through which low-income adults can earn six college credits.[3] Venture's mission is to reduce financial barriers to continuing education for adult students, help students develop literacy practices that build individual student confidence, foster whole class community, and cultivate a sense of hope for the future. OWG aims to help adult writers who've graduated from the two-semester Venture program continue (and augment) the literacy work that Venture begins in an open-ended way—that is, without necessarily moving toward a degree. OWG creates a space for adult writers with economic barriers to feel capable of and supported in accomplishing creative, professional, academic, and personal writing projects.

In order to align my IRB-approved research with OWG and also with my values and goals being involved *with/in* (rather than simply giving to) participants/communities and to seek a balanced, reciprocal relationship with others in my scholarly endeavors, I built a strong relationship with the faculty, staff, students, and alumni of Venture over 18+ months before founding OWG. During this time, I recognized that after the initial two-semester course ends, opportunities to continue writerly development and build solidarity are limited. Thus, in Spring 2020, I developed and piloted Our Writing Group (OWG) to fill this gap by providing consistent time, space, and support for program alumni to write with others. OWG represents my effort to remain true to my values and goals for research, aligning my scholarly and personal aspirations with community and stakeholder objectives to increase access, benefit, and opportunity for those involved.

As mentioned above, OWG is an optional weekly writing group for alumni of Venture with the goal to help adult undergraduates feel capable of accomplishing their writing goals. Most OWG participants are intermittently enrolled in credit-bearing postsecondary coursework; the predominantly BIPOC and low-income members of the group range in age from 20s to 60s and include gig workers, retirees, parents of grown and young children, the un- or underemployed, etc. I used the three iterative phases that typically characterize community-engaged research (Flower) to make my methodology humanizing and social justice-oriented, to strive to empower the writing group members to achieve their literacy and social goals by working *with* the writers in the group from an asset-based perspective. I aimed to make my methodology more participatory by supporting members in sharing their experiences and desires with audiences of their choosing through writing. I worked toward these goals in three main ways throughout my research with OWG:

1. OWG members and I worked to create horizontal leadership structures that aimed to set members of OWG up to maintain and sustain the writing group with or without a campus representative like me. I provided training for members on the collective leadership of the group and participated in group meetings as much as possible. However, my positionality as a professional writing instructor affiliated with the university's writing center, as well as my experience as a 'successful' student who followed a very traditional educational path and who self-identifies as a 'good' writer, position me as an 'expert' in the group. Thus, I worked to (re)define a role for myself as someone who acts on behalf of OWG to help identify and secure resources from the university and Venture to help the group continue as a space where members feel comfortable and empowered to write and share their writing.

2. My overall research with OWG endeavored to identify what kinds of practices, pedagogies, community relationships, and life experiences can help OWG participants self-identify as writers through participant-observation of OWG meetings and the *co-composition* of the meaning of multiple primary sources of information about adult undergraduate participants' writ-

ing experiences, including their stories about writing in various settings gathered through a series of semi-structured interviews, collaborative field texts written by group members, and pieces of writing written and/or shared during/ through OWG. During the 2020-2021 academic year, OWG meetings focused primarily on the writing projects of participants at three of the weekly meetings each month and specifically on conducting research (engaging in self-reflection, collaboratively composing field texts, etc.) at one weekly meeting per month. This means that the members who signed consent forms to be my co-researchers had the opportunity to write together in response to the same questions, such as "Why do I write?"; and "How is OWG affecting what and why I write, if at all?"; and "How do I want to use my writing?" in a Google Doc, being able to see and respond to what others were writing in real time (I call these Google Docs "collaborative field texts").

3. Finally, beyond the regular opportunities to work on and share their personal writing projects as well as compose field texts about their writing experiences in relation to OWG, members of the group engaged in co-analysis of their experiences and de-identified data gathered from semi-structured interviews, writing group field texts, and corresponding primary researcher memos with me by co-presenting about OWG at conferences and on campus. This practice helped me to develop collaborative codes for analysis, such as "feeling like a writer" and "writer-reader relationships." Additionally, OWG writers shared their experiences and findings during OWG readings (open to partner, community, and university stakeholders); at academic and community conferences; and in OWG student publications (circulated to partner, community, and university stakeholders online). Opportunities to share their writing, experiences, and ideas with wider audiences positioned members as experts of their own writing experiences and encouraged them to use the information gathered to take action in ways that centralize their voices (Bautista et al 2-4).

Through collaborative field texts and co-facilitation of OWG meetings, my research with OWG enabled me and members of the group to identify and investigate adult undergraduate writing topics and experiences, such as going public with one's writing and giving and receiving feedback, together. Additionally, the processes and products of this participatory action ethnography were "an ongoing attempt to place specific encounters, events, and understandings into a fuller, more meaningful context" (Tedlock 455). This article attempts to place writer's memos within OWG's community publishing efforts into a fuller, more meaningful context using data from the semi-structured interviews with OWG writers as well as writer's memos authored by participants and published in OWG's publication, *OWG Oracle*, to "reach a better understanding of the beliefs, motivations, and behaviors" that help adult undergraduate community writers in the group *feel* like writers (Tedlock 470).

Writers Need Considerate, Generous Readers to Feel Like a Writer

Participants from this study have received messages throughout their education that they are not writers, let alone good writers. Nevertheless, writing is important to them because it allows them to share their stories, make sense of their experiences, and connect with others. Importantly, the reasons for writing expressed by OWG members require generous readers/ listeners; such audiences can be invoked via writer's memos, examples of which will be given later in this piece.

Notably, all ten interviewees mentioned readers in their explanations of what helps them feel like writers. To illustrate, here are a few representative responses from semi-structured interviews with writers in OWG to the question, "Do you feel like a writer?" Echo, a 26-year-old multiracial woman, said, "Define a writer. Do I write emails? Yes. Do I write books? No. Will I write a novel? Probably not. It will be too steamy. *Fifty Shades* has nothing on me. But I don't, I don't think I'm a writer. I don't know what makes you a writer." When I replied that, in my opinion, what makes people writers is regularly engaging in the practice of writing and asked her if that changed her answer at all, she was more definitive: "No. I mean, I write, but do I— am I a writer that gets paid for it as a job? No." I proceeded to ask Echo if there were times when she felt more like a writer than others. She had to think about it. She reluctantly replied,

> I mean, once I read back on old stuff I wrote, I'm always impressed that I wrote it. Or like when [my professor] reads my work back to me, I'm like, 'Wait I wrote, I wrote that? Okay! Come through, writer.' Like once, like when I'm writing it, I don't feel any different. I feel like this is just what I write. But when someone, when I hear it in someone else's voice when they read it back, it somehow sounds, like, different. I sound smart, like when I write like, 'Huh. Okay, look at you, putting your words together like that.'

As found in previous literature (Matheiu, et al.; Norton), Echo's answers begin by connecting feeling like a writer to writing books and getting paid to write: she is not paid to write (books); therefore, she does not feel like a writer. However, she feels more like a writer when she thinks about being read.

Similarly, Dean, a 23-year-old Black man, told me:

> No, I don't feel like, I mean, [...] Does a cow feel like a cow? Like objectively, that's what you are, like, you know, you got the spots, but I don't feel. Like, I wouldn't go up to someone and say, like, I'm a writer. I'll go up to someone and say, like, I make music, or like I'm in a poetry group. But I don't go up saying, and say, like, cuz then, like, you know what I'm saying, they're just like, Where's the novel? Or like, you know what I'm saying, Do you have published work? And it's like, No, not really. And then that's kind of dismissive…

Dean knows he's a writer because he writes and shares his writing with others; however, his lack of formal publication leaves his claim of the title, "writer" open to questioning by others outside of OWG and his rap group. Overall, Dean's and Echo's answers suggest that being read helps them feel like writers. Their answers imply that their previous encounters with writers and writing have precluded anyone who isn't a *published* writer from being called a writer. Therefore, how could they confidently answer my question in the affirmative? Nevertheless, when their writing communicates, shares, and connects with others, they're able to *feel* more like writers— their writing accomplishes its aim and their writing competence grows, as Echo describes in our exchange. But when one's writing competence is questioned or dismissed, as Dean suggests, feeling like a writer becomes harder.

Echo's and Dean's reluctance is not dissimilar to how OWG participants Claudia and Sol—both poets and storytellers— answered the same question during their individual interviews; in fact, their responses shed more light on what it takes to feel like a writer for the adult undergraduates in OWG. Claudia, a white 41-year-old who was experiencing houselessness at the time of our interview, shared with me that she was "warming up to the idea" of feeling like a writer because of OWG. She explained that while she normally would not share her writing with many people, she feels more like a writer now "because [she has] people to share it with." Claudia's sense of being a writer is also at least partially dependent on sharing her work with others. In accordance with the literature on writerly self-efficacy (Bruning and Kauffman 161-162), as her readers/ listeners in OWG continue to treat her like the writer she is, instead of questioning her claim to the title due to a lack of formally published work, Claudia is more convinced that she is indeed a writer— because she writes and shares her writing with readers/listeners.

Sol, a 36-year-old Mexican mother, teacher, and activist, also feels like a writer when she has readers. She said, "Well, I feel like when I am sharing my writing with others is when I feel like a writer." However, she went on to explain that she feels like a writer specifically with readers who know what it takes to face a blank page and create something. Pointing to the importance of mastery experience— or successful writing experiences— for her writerly self-efficacy or confidence (Bruning and Kauffman 161-162), Sol explained that she experiences inner conflict when she has high expectations for herself to conform to a socially constructed idea of a writer as someone who can create something out of seemingly nothing at the drop of a hat, for any occasion, about any topic. But, as Sol says, writing and writers don't "work like that." Like Dean's response, we see how socially constructed definitions of the title writer and having an audience impact OWG participants' ability to *feel* like a writer.

Taken together, it becomes increasingly clear that the responses shared about feeling like a writer indicate these writers' levels of writerly confidence (or writerly self-efficacy) and imply that their confidence is strongly tied to reader reactions to their work. Having a generous and understanding audience for one's writing has helped enhance OWG writers' writerly self-efficacy, and therefore whether or not and how much they feel like writers. Responses like these from OWG writers about feeling like a writer support looking at writing development as nonlinear and unpredictable because it is informed by complex interactions between various motives, challenges, and opportunities for writing over time, which in turn inform writing practices, models, and skills that vary from person to person (Bazerman, et al.). They also highlight how the development of one's writerly identity, their ability to *feel* like a writer, is influenced by what that individual needs and wants from writing. Members of OWG need and want considerate readers to *feel* like writers.

The next section details how OWG writers engage with their readers through a specific writing genre—the writer's memo—as a means of actively developing their own understanding and identity as a writer. Our community publishing efforts in OWG aim to elicit the considerate, generous readings OWG writers need and want by including writer's memos that serve as accompaniments to the poetry, personal essays, short stories, and other work that grace the pages of OWG's semiannual publication, *OWG Oracle*. Writer's memos can explain the purpose of a piece, why it was written, and what the author hopes the piece will achieve for readers. They are meant to help orient readers to a piece, give them important background information, and/or simply explain what inspired the writer. They also help members of OWG speak to their readers on their own terms via direct address. OWG writers invoke their readers in these memos, and this seemingly simple act actually positions these writers as aware and in charge of their own meanings and intentions.

Writer's Memos: Invitations to Read and Be Read

OWG's participant publication, *OWG Oracle*, is published in the winter and spring of each academic year. It is meant to reflect the ethos of OWG. As a collection of poetry, personal essays, short stories, and excerpts from larger works addressing a wide variety of topics as well as corresponding writer's memos, *OWG Oracle* is participant-driven. Everyone in the group can submit to the publication, and every piece submitted is workshopped and accepted for publication. Members choose their works; choose what editorial suggestions from me and other group members to take and which ones to disregard; and describe the purpose of each piece, why it was written, and what the author hopes the piece will achieve for readers in corresponding writer's memos.

Through participants' writer's memos, each issue of *OWG Oracle* coached readers into examining and perhaps even disregarding their expectations of published writing, of "established" writers. Rachel Jackson and Dorothy Whitehorse DeLaune's concept of "community listening" is useful for conceptualizing how the members of OWG invoked readers with the writing they chose to publish and their corresponding writer's memos. Community listening is "a literate act that engages listeners as collaborators in meaning making across multiple sites" where "listeners work together with storytellers to construct and sustain cultural knowledge by building storied connections across difference" (Jackson & DeLaune 41). The predominantly BIPOC, low-income writers in OWG engaged their readers as collaborators in making meaning through their writer's memos, thereby acknowledging and even leveraging the fact that they come from different intersectional positionalities than their readers. For example, Sol's writer's memo for her piece "Although the Cage is Made of Gold, It is Still a Prison" challenged readers to "put themselves in the shoes of the undocumented immigrant." In so doing, Sol constructed the experiential knowledge of the undocumented immigrant as similar to the experiential knowledge of worry we all gained during the COVID-19 pandemic, and as such, she worked to build connections across difference.

It helped OWG writers use their writer's memos more purposefully to think of the memos as a chance to directly address readers of their work. Here are some examples:

- In Song's memo for "A Reason to Smile," she explained to readers that the poem was meant to reflect her belief in the power of "a simple smile" to "warm someone's heart, make their day or even save a life."
- In Puff's memo for a poem entitled "Passing Off Normal," she challenged readers to rethink what's considered normal through a trip to the zoo.
- The writer's memo for Miz's piece "(taste)percep-tion" asked readers questions to help them think about how empathy can change our perception of feelings and actions in an effort to help readers think about how they feel and act in a different way.
- Heaven's writer's memo for "The Sound of My Relaxation" acknowledged that everyone relaxes differently and encouraged readers to think about how they relax in terms of sounds.
- Claudia's writer's memo for "The Skins I Shed as an Isabella Tiger Moth" mentioned her specific consideration of people's familiarity with wooly bear caterpillars.

Importantly, none of the above examples are my own analyses of these writers' works; they are the writers' own characterizations of what aims their pieces accomplish and what authorial decisions they made that helped them accomplish those aims. In articulating these authorial decisions and aims, OWG participants position themselves as empowered over their own meanings and intentions.

This important collaboration between OWG writers and their readers couldn't be done without community publishing because when one's writing is published, it lasts, it can travel, it has a farther reach than it would if it had stayed in a notebook or on a personal device. Community publishing is important to helping writers make meaning on their own terms; as previously indicated, publication, broadly speaking, and more specifically the pedagogical practice of composing and sharing writer's memos bolster mastery experience and social persuasion (Bruning and Kauffman)— they signify success in writing and a belief in an author's writerly potential for both writers in the act of choosing to publish their work and readers in the act of collaborating with writers to arrive at shared meaning. I see this use of *OWG Oracle* writer's memos as reflective of OWG writers taking greater ownership of their texts and the work they want their pieces to do for readers (Parks 525; Mathieu et al. 10) because writer's memos encourage intentional reflection on their writing.

Rather than a push-pull (Smitherman) between what you do as a writer and what a classroom or academic discourse community (or even a particular reader) might expect of you as a writer, OWG writers fostered their own community that made our writing values and the purposes of our published pieces clear to anyone and everyone in their memos. I sought to highlight this and support the writers' work across difference in the editor's letters I wrote for each issue where I called attention to readers' expectations of writers, in the general sense of the term, and encouraged them to shed those expectations by championing each writer's individual voice as well as their own writing conventions and intentional writerly decisions: "Thus, I encourage you, dear readers, to read each piece with special attention to the voice of each writer. Those commas, capitalized words, ellipses, emojis, periods and lack thereof are meant to be there to guide you to hear— no listen— to each piece in the way it was meant to reach you." In essence, the writer's memos and editor's letters in *OWG Oracle* encourage readers to pay attention to and value "the wisdom that comes to us intuitively" (Okun) while reading each entry.

I assert that the writing and publishing of writer's memos alongside each entry in *OWG Oracle* helps the adult undergraduates in OWG *feel* like writers because they put the writers themselves in charge of their own meanings and intentions, and writer's memos give writers the opportunity to clearly articulate those meanings and intentions to their readers. Furthermore, writer's memos encourage writers to consider their own intersectional experiences as readers, and actively work to build affirming meaning-making relationships with readers. To take this control, to wield the power of being a *published* writer in this constructive way, not only demonstrates OWG writers' writerly prowess (thereby enhancing their writerly self-efficacy) but also showcases how writers and readers can work together to revise socially constructed notions of who gets to read and be read.

For example, by explaining to readers the purpose of, inspiration for, and rhetorical/ literary strategies used in a piece in their memos, writers in OWG did not make assumptions about what readers do and do not know. For example, Dean's writer's memo for "I arm wrestled racism" went into deep detail about the WWE wrestling match that inspired his poem. By explaining these things to their readers, members of OWG published in *OWG Oracle* demonstrate that it's okay for readers to not share their same experiences, background knowledge, etc. Instead, Dean pulled the curtain back on the WWE wrestling match he watched to help readers better enjoy his instructive poem. When OWG writers made moves like this in their writer's memos, they demonstrated that their writing is not just for their personal benefit but to benefit the community of readers their pieces reach. Claudia's memo for "Letter to Squanto" did this by sharing what she learned from a particular group meeting: she specifically mentioned using terms introduced during a session facilitated by Heaven about Thanksgiving and the Wampanoag Indians throughout her piece. Overall, the writer's memos made clear that the pieces in each issue of *OWG Oracle* were written by individuals who have intersectional identities that influence what they write and how they write it. The information shared in writer's memos clarifies that each piece is reflective of individual experiences and ideas helping level the playing field between the writers and any readers who may have different experiences and ideas.

Some OWG writers directly asked readers if certain rhetorical moves were successful and clarified the intent behind their pieces of writing in their writer's memos. For instance, Sol asked if readers were successfully transported to her wedding day in her memo for "Lipstick." In so doing, OWG writers established a more equitable and un-hierarchized relationship with their readers; they acknowledged that the success of their piece depends on both the reader and the writer— that the success of their piece was not only under the control of the writer. This relates back to OWG writers' reasons for writing, which include to connect and share with others. The *OWG Oracle* writer's memos emphasize connections and collaboration between readers and writers. This can be seen in Song's encouragement for readers to let her story inspire them to dream, be creative, and get their rewards in her memo for "Symphony Boyd's Award."

Finally, OWG writer's memos can directly engage readers in a discussion about emotions. I found this especially apparent in Miz's writer's memos, which explicitly engaged with feelings of fear, love, and doubt. For example, in her writer's memo for "Out my Wind-ow," Miz wrote, "In this poem, I'm asking you what the view is like, what's it like? What exactly is your interpretation of my window? My view is fogged; I do not see myself the way you see me: I love that and it saddens me." The memos in *OWG Oracle* explicitly worked against the disembodiment of words, ideas, and language from writers (and readers), and instead articulated and embraced the contexts that inspired each piece. As Miz wrote later in that same memo,

> I have transitioned between various stages of self and the process continues to fascinate me. When a piece like this comes from a deeply humbling and painful process, it is beautiful to release, but more so, healing. This interpretation of myself no longer blocks the window OR my view AND the older version of me is no longer welcome to view. What is left is the imagination.

Therefore, writing and publishing writer's memos in *OWG Oracle* helped members of OWG make strides toward kinder, more inclusive understandings of writers and writing that do not rely on hard and fast rules nor engage in hierarchized power dynamics through invocations of readers who were open, inclusive, and willing to meet writers where they were. And this is an empowering exercise: it yields "self-esteem, self-confidence, potential creativity and spontaneity," as linguist Neville Alexander has written about (quoted in Baker-Bell 27). Publishing these memos alongside their entries in *OWG Oracle* empowered writers in OWG to share those more inclusive understandings of writers and writing with larger audiences, positioning them as rhetorically savvy authors. Via sharing their own thoughts, experiences, intentions, and questions in their memos, OWG writers engaged in acts of vulnerability that served as a foundation for building affirming meaning-making relationships with their readers. These affirming reader-writer relationships positively recast socially constructed ideas of who can read and write.

Conclusion

In this article, I've explained how OWG's community publishing efforts help the writing group's adult undergraduates *feel* like writers by providing opportunities for them to invoke and interact with readers in an affirming, equitable way through writer's memos. Data from the semi-structured interviews with OWG members suggest what helps these adult undergraduate community writers feel like writers are generous and considerate readers. The examples from participants' writer's memos shared in this piece indicate how these writers instantiate such readers. This is further supported by data from collaborative field texts written by group members: OWG writers mention writing for others who feel challenged by society, others who are interested in political issues and equity, "the survivors of the world who were silenced and are now lost and found" (March 2021 Collaborative Field Text). Many times, OWG members expressed a desire to write for anyone who would read/ listen, and they understand their audiences to be "people like me and people like you. Anybody who appreciates writing, either written or vocalized and has a heart is who I write for" (March 2021 Collaborative Field Text). So, in addition to writing for other OWG members, their family, and their friends, writers in the group describe their audience as "any and everyone that desire change because we all dream and have faith for a better tomorrow" (April 2021 Collaborative Field Text). When they write for such audiences, they not only see themselves in their readers but can also exercise power as writers to connect with readers unlike them via their writer's memos. To exercise this power of being a *published* writer in this constructive way demonstrates OWG writers' writerly prowess, helping them *feel* like writers. Furthermore, this practice showcases how writers and readers can work together to revise socially constructed notions of who gets to read and be read, enacting important social change via community publishing.

Thus, through writing and publishing writer's memos alongside each of their pieces, members learn about themselves as writers, and upon learning about themselves as writers, OWG members more confidently self-identify as writers. As writers, then, they can create texts with social weight— texts that accomplish their goals, texts that can create change— and confidently share those texts with wider audiences, thereby undermining previous messages they received that implied that more, better, or different literacies can transform their lives (Graff). Instead, the literacies that writers bring to the group are enough; they are worthy of publication. OWG and its *Oracle* create space for adult writers with economic barriers to contribute to the world of writing by advocating for transformed perceptions of "good" writing and writers in their interactions within the group as well as their writer's memos specifically and their community publishing more broadly. That is, when discussing *why* we were publishing work and our identity and ethos as a group of writers, many members expressed a desire to "be real" with their work, to challenge readers to "transcend" judgment, to "be the future." This is not to say that OWG writers did not struggle to find a balance between being authentic, knowing that all writers make mistakes, and wanting *OWG Oracle* to be taken seriously by others with more stereotypical expectations. In the end, however, OWG writer Miz made a point about seeing "the survivor" in language with accents, pauses, typos, etc., and Dean pointed out that OWG is not a *class* with strict standards or curricular requirements, but a *community writing group* where the only mandates for their writing are the ones individuals impose on themselves. Thus, writing groups and community publications like ours offer opportunities to gain more confidence around the writing we produce and the processes we take to produce it. That is, Our Writing Group is a space where our unique individual writing processes are not only accepted, but celebrated – and where our writing products are treated as important manifestations and representations of the identities and values we want to put out into the world.

I interpret these desires for the writing published in *OWG Oracle* as enacting the orientation change urged by writing studies scholar Steve Parks, who recommends moving from exchange value (or the exchange of one text for another) to use value (or value being determined by a communal process to determine a literacy product's use) in community publishing (524). Rather than simply wanting to put out a publication, the reflection prompted by composing writer's memos to accompany each of their pieces helped members of OWG decide how they wanted their publication to be used, what values it would espouse, and accordant editorial decisions. Thus, this orientation change has helped OWG develop a "model of aesthetic and cultural production that not only provides alternative cultural products for use inside and outside our classrooms, but also alternative systems of production for our students and community partners" (Parks 516). That is, the biannual publications are founded on a belief in "the right of communities to create their own aesthetic self-definitions" and serve to "[expand] access to the means of [literate] production" (Parks 516). OWG writers are in control of how they go public, what they go public with, why they go public, and take advantage of opportunities to learn how to do this public work themselves as a collective. Putting the power to go public in the hands of OWG writers themselves helps OWG revalue publication and the title *writer*, moving it from something only outside readers/ listeners determine to something that is collaboratively achieved between writers and readers. Such a reorientation to publishing one's writing helps empower OWG writers to go public with their writing on their own terms, which in turn helps enhance their writerly self-efficacy and encourages them to *feel* like writers.

Showcasing their work through publication and the explanatory space provided by writer's memos is one way that helps members of OWG feel like writers. This pedagogical practice helped the members of OWG build and demonstrate skills, knowledges, and discourses regarding writing and stimulated their active and positive invocation of and engagement with considerate, generous readers. I contend that the writer's memos authored by participants and published in *OWG Oracle* amplified the positive effects community publishing can have on writerly self-efficacy. OWG and *OWG Oracle* are opportunities for multiply-marginalized adult undergraduate writers to directly interact with their readers— to share their insights, truths, experiences, and lives with others through their writing. Members' writer's memos reveal that writers in Our Writing Group are intentionally arranging their words on the page to achieve desired effects, opening space and dialogue for readers to appreciate and interpret alongside the writers themselves. Thus, including writer's memos in community publishing efforts can have positive implications for writers themselves and reader-writer relationships in community writing, indicating that this pedagogical practice is useful beyond the composition classroom. The publication of writer's memos provides an important opportunity for writers to be recognized by themselves and others as just that: writers.

Notes

1. I recognize and acknowledge that there is other important work in Writing Studies that helps us better understand adult writers' needs, desires, experiences, and even self-efficacy; however, I do not delve into that body of work because it is beyond the focus of this article, which is to explore the potential of *writer's memos in community publishing* for multiply-marginalized adult writers.

2. All names used in this article are pseudonyms, including Quest and Our Writing Group (OWG). Participants of the writing group chose their own pseudonyms while I chose the pseudonyms for the group, our community partner, and all others.

3. To apply for admission into the Venture program, a prospective student must be at least 18 years old, have a high school diploma or GED/HSED, and demonstrate financial need (income at or near the federal poverty level).

Works Cited

Baker-Bell, April. *Linguistic Justice: Black Language, Literacy, Identity, and Pedagogy.* Routledge, 2020.

Bautista, M A, et al. "Participatory Action Research and City Youth: Methodological Insights from the Council of Youth Research." *Teachers College Record*, vol. 115, no. 10, 2013, pp. 1–23.

Bazerman, Charles, et al. *The Lifespan Development of Writing.* National Council of Teachers of English, 2018.

Bruning, Roger H., and Douglas F. Kauffman. "Self-Efficacy Beliefs and Motivation in Writing Development." *Handbook of Writing Research, Second Edition*, edited by Steve Graham, et al., Guilford Publications, 2015, pp. 160-173.

Byrd, Antonio. "Between Learning and Opportunity: A Study of African American Coders' Networks of Support." *Literacy in Composition Studies*, vol. 7, no. 2, 2019, pp. 31-56. DOI: 10.21623/1.7.2.3.

Flower, Linda. *Community Literacy and the Rhetoric of Public Engagement.* Southern Illinois University Press, 2008, https://muse.jhu.edu/book/22615.

Guest, Sara, et al. "Respect, Writing, Community: Write Around Portland." *Circulating Communities: the Tactics and Strategies of Community Publishing*, edited by Paula Mathieu et al., Lexington Books, 2012, pp. 49–69.

Graff, Harvey J. *The Literacy Myth: Literacy and Social Structure in the Nineteenth-Century City.* Academic Press, 1982.

Greenberg, Daphne. "The Challenges Facing Adult Literacy Programs." *Community Literacy Journal*, vol. 3, no. 1, 2008, pp. 39–54, doi:10.25148/clj.3.1.009480.

Jackson, Rachel C. & Dolores DeLaune. "Decolonizing Community Writing With Community Listening: Story, Transrhetorical Resistance, and Indigenous Cultural Literacy Activism." *Community Literacy Journal*, vol. 13, no. 1, p. 37–54, 2018.

Lundberg, Carol, et al. "Sources of Social Support and Self-Efficacy for Adult Students." *Journal of College Counseling*, vol. 11, 2008, pp. 58–72.

Mathieu, Paula, et al. *Circulating Communities the Tactics and Strategies of Community Publishing.* Lexington Books, 2012.

Miller Brown, Sherry. "Strategies That Contribute to Nontraditional/ Adult Student Development and Persistence." *PAACE Journal of Lifelong Learning*, vol. 11, 2002, pp. 67–76.

Norton, Sue. "All the World's a Page: Towards a Definition of 'Writer' in an Age of Opportunity." *American, British, & Canadian Studies*, vol. 25, no. 1, 2015, pp. 3-8. Sciendo, https://doi.org/10.1515/abcsj-2015-0004.

Okun, Tema. "CHARACTERISTICS." *White Supremacy Culture*, 2021, https://www.whitesupremacyculture.info/characteristics.html. Accessed 22 June 2022.

Pajares, Frank, and Gio Valiante. "Self-Efficacy Beliefs and Motivation in Writing Development." *Handbook of Writing Research*, First Edition, edited by Charles A. MacArthur, et al., Guilford Publications, 2006.

Parks, Steven J. "Strategic Speculations on the Question of Value: The Role of Community Publishing in English Studies." *College English*, vol. 71, no. 5, 2009, pp. 506-527. JSTOR, https://www.jstor.org/stable/25652988.

Perry, Kristen H., et al. "The 'Ofcourseness' of Functional Literacy: Ideologies in Adult Literacy." *Journal of Literacy Research*, vol. 50, no. 1, Mar. 2018, pp. 74–96, doi:10.1177/1086296X17753262.

Restaino, Jessica, and Laurie Cella. *Unsustainable: Re-Imagining Community Literacy, Public Writing, Service-Learning and the University*. Lexington Books, 2012.

Rosenberg, Lauren. "'You Have to Knock at the Door for the Door Get Open': Alternative Literacy Narratives and the Development of Textual Agency in Writing by Newly Literate Adults." *Community Literacy Journal*, vol. 2, no. 2, 2008, pp. 113–44, doi:10.25148/clj.2.2.009495.

Schrantz, James Lee. "Teaching Composition to Nontraditional Students: Intertextuality and Textual Development." Texas Christian University, 1995.

Smitherman, Geneva. *Word From the Mother: Language and African Americans*. Routledge, 2006.

Sommers, Jeffrey. "The Writer's Memo: Collaboration, Response, and Development." *Writing and Response: Theory, Practice, and Research*, National Council of Teachers of English, Urbana, IL, 1989, pp. 174–186.

"Submissions Guidelines." *Community Literacy Journal*, University of Denver/ Coalition for Community Writing, digitalcommons.fiu.edu/communityliteracy/styleguide.html. Accessed 9 Aug. 2024.

Tedlock, Barbara. "Ethnography & Ethnographic Representation." *Handbook of Qualitative Research*, edited by Norman Denzin and Yvonna Lincoln, 2nd ed., Sage Publications, 2000, pp. 455–486.

"The Writer's Memo." *Teach Write Now*, National Writing Project, teach.nwp.org/the-writers-memo/. Accessed 6 Aug. 2024.

Wardle, Elizabeth, and Linda Adler-Kassner, editors. *Naming What We Know: Threshold Concepts of Writing Studies*. Utah State University Press, 2015.

Wells, Jaclyn M. "Investigating Adult Literacy Programs through Community Engagement Research: A Case Study." *Community Literacy Journal*, vol. 8, no. 2, 2014, pp. 49–66, doi:10.25148/clj.8.2.009310.

Author Bio

Gabrielle Isabel Kelenyi (she/her) is an Assistant Professor of English at Lafayette College in Easton, PA. She earned her PhD in Composition and Rhetoric at University of Wisconsin-Madison where her community-engaged research focused on community literacies and writerly self-efficacy. Gabbi's current research interests include anti-racism and activism in writing; composition pedagogy; and community literacies. At Lafayette, she enjoys teaching about the field of Writing Studies, including how community engagement manifests across sub-disciplines in the field.

Coda: Community Writing and Creative Work

Editors' Introduction: An Alphabet of Resistance

Gabrielle Kelenyi, Chad Seader, Alison Turner, and Stephanie Wade

In lieu of a traditional introduction to our spring 2025 issue, Coda offers An Alphabet of Resistance to draw attention to words the federal government has removed from their websites.[1] We see the removal of these words as acts of harm that require us to resist. We aim to amplify these words because words–in general and these in particular– allow us to name our experiences, to critique systems of oppression, to engage in research, to imagine better worlds, to build relationships, and to create structures to bring better worlds into being.

Interspersed among the words, we introduce the work in this issue of Coda.

An Alphabet of Resistance

A is for accessible, activism, activists, advocacy, advocate, advocates, affirming care, all-inclusive, allyship, anti-racism, antiracist, assigned at birth, assigned female at birth, assigned male at birth, at risk

B is for barrier, barriers, belong, bias, biased, biased toward, biases, biases towards, biologically female, biologically male, BIPOC, Black, breastfeed + people, breastfeed + person

C is for chestfeed + people, chestfeed + person, clean energy, climate crisis, climate science, **and Coda,** who states these words. we restate them. we draw your attention to them so you, too, use them, so we don't lose them, so we maintain our ability to critique systems of oppression, (so we don't lose what these words stand for), so we honor the experiences they name, we support the research they allow, we imagine better worlds and build relationships and create structures to bring better worlds into being; commercial sex worker, community diversity, community equity, confirmation bias, cultural competence, cultural differences, cultural heritage, cultural sensitivity, culturally appropriate, culturally responsive

D is for DEI, DEIA, DEIAB, DEIJ, disabilities, disability, discriminated, discrimination, discriminatory, disparity, diverse, diverse backgrounds, diverse communities, diverse community, diverse group, diverse groups, diversified, diversify, diversifying, diversity

---

1. For more about the removal of these words, see Diane Ravitch's March 8, 2025, blog post, which includes a link to the *New York Times* article from March 7th that reported the original story.

E is for enhance the diversity, enhancing diversity, environmental quality, equal opportunity, equality, equitable, equitableness, equity, ethnicity, excluded, exclusion, expression

F is for female, females, feminism, fostering inclusivity; and **"Freedom is Fundamental" by S. M. Foysol Ahmed, Heather Cleary, and Gwendolyn Hooks**, which presents a set of three poems that came out of a time-limited community empathy writing project. The poems are connected yet disparate, creating a sense that they come from the same community writing project but could also stand on their own. "In the Silence" takes you to a place where dreams hang in the balance, while "The Assumption" seems to describe what's at stake when they do. And "Answers" makes us question the utility of our dreams in the first place

G is for GBV, gender, gender based, gender based violence, gender diversity, gender identity, gender ideology, gender-affirming care, genders, Gulf of Mexico

H is for hate speech, health disparity, health equity, hispanic minority, historically, and **"How We See Free" by Debbie Allen, Susann Moeller, Chuck Salmons, Rikki Santer, and Karen Scott**, a collaborative contrapuntal poem created by participants at the Ohio Underground Railroad Whistle-Stop Poetry Tour who responded to the prompt "What does freedom mean to you?"

I is for identity, immigrants, implicit bias, implicit biases, inclusion, inclusive, inclusive leadership, inclusiveness, inclusivity, increase diversity, increase the diversity, indigenous community, inequalities, inequality, inequitable, inequities, inequity, injustice, institutional; and **"(the) intersection" by The Moonlight Cheese Alliance and Leslee N. Johnson**, a zine which emerged from a grant-funded partnership with Burners without Borders to support the communities in Asheville, North Carolina after Hurricane Helen, a testament to the generative power of community to build hope and create meaning after tragedy; and intersectional, intersectionality

J is for Jewish people who support Palestine, **K is for** key groups, key people, key populations, **L is for** Latinx, LGBT, LGBTQ, **M is for** marginalize, marginalized, men who have sex with men, mental health, minorities, minority, most risk, MSM, multicultural, Mx, **N is for** Native American, non-binary, Nonbinary, **O is for** oppression, oppressive, orientation

P is for "(The) Peach Tree" by Calley Marotta, a story that centers overlapping communities comprised of people, places, and a peach tree. In doing so, the story also represents the relationships and meanings that emerge from these communities, relationships that point to new ways of being and living. As the author notes: "This work has been deeply influenced by traditions of Black Feminism and womanism and Disability Justice…movements that encourage writers not to settle for the world that is but dream the world that might be" and people + uterus, people-centered care, person-centered, person-centered care; **"Plantulary" by Sequoia Hauck, Rachel Jendrzejewski, Koa Mirai, Mankwe Ndosi, Lela Pierce,**

Pramila Vasudevan, and Jeffrey Wells, a word list that is experimental and multi-vocal, inviting and challenging readers to alter not only their perspectives on nature, but also the ways they commune with it. Slow down and speed up with Aniccha Arts' contemplation and interpretation of the ways of native and non-native plants in South Minneapolis neighborhoods; polarization, political, pollution; and **"(The) Pond" by Joonna Smitherman Trapp,** a poem that, having emerged from a writing retreat, serves as a reflection on the retreat itself and the roles of spiritual retreat and engagement; and pregnant people, pregnant person, pregnant persons, prejudice, privilege, privileges, promote diversity, promoting diversity, pronoun, pronouns, prostitute

Q is for ask questions, **R is for** race, race and ethnicity, racial, racial diversity, racial identity, racial inequality, racial justice, racially, racism

S is for segregation, sense of belonging, sex, sexual preferences, sexuality, social justice, sociocultural, socioeconomic; and **"(The) Sound You Never Forget" by Ania Payne**, where she remembers her first semester teaching community-engaged courses and the boundaries she needed to push to do so (from letting a dog in the building to acknowledging a relative lack of control when working with community partners). Using humor and serious reflection as a bridge between business writing students with organizations working in the community around them, Payne writes pathways for community-engaged teaching that is unpredictable, imperfect, and worth every minute; and status, stereotype, stereotypes, systemic, systemically

T is for they/them, trans, transgender, transsexual, trauma, traumatic, Tribal; and **"Two Poems by Three Authors" by Bonnie Vidrine-Isbell, Aurora Matzke, Genesea Carter,** who initially collaborated on academic pieces about the work of writing program administration. They exercise their collective third voice in poetry as well, a process that, they explain, allows them to be vulnerable, to feel safe, to attend to their bodies, and to play. In the resulting poems, their third voice offers a meditation on structure and agency by contrasting order and excess

U is for unconscious bias, underappreciated, underprivileged, underrepresentation, underrepresented, underserved, undervalued, **V is for** victim, victims, vulnerable populations

W is for women, women and underrepresented; and **"#WeAllWrite/We All Right" by Tabitha Espina and Kelvin Keown,** a demonstration of the writing that can materialize from community-driven writing projects. Part exquisite corpse poem, part crowd-sourced reflections on writing, this piece pulls the curtain back on the culture of writing at an Asian American and Native American Pacific Islander-Serving Institution. Espina and Keown's images celebrate writing and its ubiquity

X, Y, Z

Plantulary

Sequoia Hauck, Rachel Jendrzejewski, Koa Mirai, Mankwe Ndosi, Lela Pierce, Pramila Vasudevan, and Jeffrey Wells

Reflection for Aniccha Arts' Plantulary Word List

Aniccha Arts (est. 2004) is an experimental arts collaborative based in Mni Sota Makoce. Under the leadership of Pramila Vasudevan, our group has involved a number of artists over the years. *Plantulary* was our most recent production, featuring a live performance grounded in a word list that was generated over the course of a year. Held at Minneapolis's Red Eye Theater in December 2024, *Plantulary* reminded us as artists to stay connected to our ecology through language and embodiment. To rehearse, we took plant walks through South Minneapolis neighborhoods, contemplating our presence on Dakota land with our complex and diverse personal histories. Rather than relying on Google or plant-identifying apps as our mediators to engage with plant beings around us, we worked with live interactions and learned about the ways of native and non-native plants. We came up with words and embodied gestures that describe what we observed and sensed, which make up this *Plantulary* word list. In this way, our performance became an accumulation of those observations as we deepened our relationship with plants that nourished our perspectives.

For example, we created the phrase, "needle roll - S P I N N N N N N N N in the fingers" in late spring when we encountered a tall pine tree on a plant walk. When we rolled a pine needle from this tree back and forth across the thumbpad, there was an ease about that connection that was notably grounding in the body. We found ourselves continuously moving the needles across both thumb pads, and these gestures catalyzed into other movements throughout the body, creating very lovely short dances. Then, in the process of documenting needle roll and its definition in what would become our word list, we wanted to capture the particular qualities we observed of the tree that day, as reflected in our text-rendering of the multiple Ns.

At the performance, we distributed the word list below to all audience members as testament to our process of being attuned to plants, trees, and non-human living things. The vocabulary on this list was woven into and throughout the performance itself, which involved dancing and singing. To continue the example of "needle roll," two of us sang this phrase and accompanying definition from the back corner of the stage; we then began moving in a patterned way towards the audience, inviting theatergoers into the process. While we did not cover every word, the performance highlighted specific words from each season (loosely defined), whether it was spring ("Warburbling"), summer ("Loudpour"), or fall ("Crispedraw").

Plantulary

Waburbling (April 7 – May 22, 2024)

needle roll - S P I N N N N N N N N in the fingers

arm drape - hang arms   <   W   I   D   E   >   (sag) (weep)

burr budding - presshandsagainstjointswith !!!!!! sudden emergence of fingers !!!!!!

mossing|lichening - sssssssslllllloooooooooowwwwwlllllyyyyyyyeeeexxxxxppppppaaaaaannnnnddddddddd aaaaaaaaccccccrrrrrrrooooooooossssssss aaaaaaa sssssuuuuuurrrrrrrrffffffffffaaaaaaaaccccccccceeeeeeee

tapping - ~ SEARCH FOR WATER WITH YOUR FOOT ~

edging - ||| SEARCH SURFACES find the space between restriction and destruction |||

fuffing - (cupyourhandsaroundyourface): fist to wide fingers spread out

budaging - s///////////u/////r/////////g////e//////// with hand>inside>hand traveling _O U T W A R D_

polyskansing - ** DANCE IN SIMULTANEITY! ALL TOGETHER NOW! **

saprun - mark with fingers saprunningdownyourbody

solayering - make the {{{{{{{{{{inside of your body}}}}}}}}}} solid as the }}}}}}}}}}} outside of your body {{{{{{{{{{ sssss " h " i " f " t " sssss

greennogreen - express awe of -AND- aversion to $$$ viridescence $$$ with your whole body; move closer to then move away then move closer to then move away then move closer to then move away (repeat indefinitely)

bunchy - :::::: squishtogetherlikeberriesorbuds :::::: (within your own self, or together with others)

limbing - activate bunchy, but only with —--- arms —--- & —--- legs —--- (within your own self, or together with others)

plepleplepleple - \\s}{h}{i}{m}{e}{r// your body in conversation with the wind }}}}}}}}}}}}}}}}

truncated - be still +++++++++++++ be connected to something else

VY - find every 'V' and 'Y' in your body

scentipeding - gather with others >< keep your eyes slightly open >< let the leader follow the scent >>>>>> become the leader following the scent

drippy drips - T A P S C R A P E P A T R U B G L I D E S C R A T C H your finger across surfaces

pushout - PRESS! STRETCH! PROPEL! REACH! into an ======= e x p a n d e d ======= spirit-body

grow up grow down - use your WHOLE BODY (you know what to do, don't overthink it)

radiate out - \s.c-a%t#t=e;r   e~m~i~t   b___e___a___m   (on the floor)

twisty turvying - consider what is possible with only `a`r`m`s` and 'h'a'n'd's'

potenting - sit, hand-on-head, pressing-mouth: A   I   R

flaking - peeeeeeeeeel & reveeeeeeeeeal all around yourself, or around another person's limbs

Loudpour (June 18 – September 20, 2024)

    chemical warding - ~~~~~ P R O T E C T Y O U R E N E R G Y ~~~~~

      accelerated growing - fastforward to the next generation !!!!!!!

        vinding - scAFFOLD wItH oTHERS

          crowding - growww in the //////////// same space \\\\\\\\\\\\\\\\ as everybody else

            plantsistence - *** I | N | S | I | S | T on L | I | V | I | N | G ***

              plantyielding - become a scaffold become the earth

                fightordance - move from a place of ;;;F;R;I;C;T;I;O;N;;;

                  pinnating - embody a loooooooooooooooooooooooooooooooooooooong stem with little leaves

                    palmating - ^a^r^r^a^n^g^e^ ^y^o^u^r^ ^l^e^a^v^e^s^ ^l^i^k^e^ ^t^h^e^ ^p^a^l^m^ ^o^f^ ^a^ ^h^a^n^d^

                  tunneling - presswrigglepushthrough |BRICKANDMORTAR|

                moss archepelagoing - (be a soft tiny island on a wall)

                  moss peel - [hold] [yourself] [together] as you peellllllll offfff a surface..........

                  moss painting - _____ flatten yourself into a single layer

                lichen splatting - BURST! COLOR!! ONTO A VERTICAL WALL!!!

                ivy reach - extendddddddddddddddddddddddddddddddddddddddddddddddddd

                ivy pile - cuddle-layer-dwell (on top of each other)

                chromo fomo hypno mezmo - c H a N g E h O w Y o U r E y E s S e E c O l O r {{{like clumpsofblackeyedsusans}}}

                growing upside down - >in^vert< your *petals* and your \stems\

                green carpeting - ||| TAKE OVER THE AREA WITH DENSE BEING, DENSE JOY |||

                pillowing - F F F F F F F F I I I I I I I I L L L L L L L L L L L L L L L O O O O U U U T T T T

                lush - lean into your a—b—u—n—dance

                crisping edges - ### allow yourself ### to age ### without resistance >>>>>>>>>>>>>>>>>

                summer plepleple - *** i *** n *** h *** a *** l *** e *** to an !?! expanded state !?!

                plant walk - go outside go inside go outside go inside go outside

                windpressing - lightly but firmly make an <<<||||IMPRINT|||>>> on the)f o l i a g e(

Crispedraw (September 21 – December 17, 2024)

                crisping (see also: crisping edges) - move inward ### let yourself ### be dry and brittle ###

                  quietning - consolidateyourself

              evergreening - [[[find a different framework ,,inside,, what's happening all around you]]]

                  redding - <<<< **** warming of leaves ****** >>>>

          lifeathing - fully let go ——————— articulate contradictions () binaries () possibilities

              rigor memory - &//&}} be the remnant structure of a living plant {{&//&

              moonearing - find A L L L L L the ways (you) S E N S E and R E S P O N D

                flumping - f a l l & shrivel _-_-_-_-_-_ from first frost

              rooing - }}peek out}} of the dirt like a carrot; feel the """*W*O*N*D*E*R*"""

abloomboom - >#>#>#> !!! HERALD THE NEW SEASON LOUDLY @@@ IN A LOW SLOW GRAND VOICE <#<#<#<

            dinonamic (opposite of flumping) - STAND STRONG + FIRM + RESILIENT AS KALE IN THE COLD

hodgepod - let the #(&$)#&$)(#*&$)(*&#$|| W I N D //)#(*$_#)*&$)(*#&$)(*#&$ bring you))together((with other seeds into a clump

          seedsaddle - strAteGicAllY >>>>///////////———— mOvE >>>>///////////———— and pLaCe YoURsElf ... like seeds ...

Acknowledgments

Thank you to Jasmine Kar Tang, the *Plantulary* collaborators, Pillsbury House Theater, MOVO, Red Eye Theater, and family and friends for supporting the development and production of *Plantulary*.

Author Bios

Sequoia Hauck (they/them) is a two-spirit, queer, Anishinaabe and Hupa filmmaker, interdisciplinary artist and director who creates work that indigenizes the process of art-making. Their work weaves Indigenous epistemologies, indigiqueer identity and the possibilities of Indigenous futurism. Sequoia is a 2023 Jerome Hill Artist Fellow and First Peoples Fund Cultural Capital Fellow as well as an Aniccha Arts Artistic Associate. www.sequoiahauck.com

Rachel Jendrzejewski (she/her) is a writer who frequently collaborates with choreographers, musicians, and visual artists to interrogate language and unpack wide-ranging performative vocabularies. She is grateful to be part of the Plantulary cohort and a rhizome of conversations and collaborations extending from it. Recent works have included a\c|c/e|p\t|i/n|s\i|s/t, an exhibition created with Pramila Vasudevan at Hair+Nails Gallery (2022); a writing vector on deep pattern for Valerie Oliveiro's VASTNESSESS (2024); and TRACES (AFTER SOPHIE CALLE), an immersive performance created with WaxFactory, featuring matt regan and Jeffrey Wells, among others, presented by Walker Art Center (2024). Rachel is a Co-Artistic Director at Red Eye (on medical leave), a Playwrights' Center Core Writer, and a student of cancer and plants.

Koa Mirai (she/they), a cultural anthropologist by training, dedicates their work to empowering BIPOC real estate developers to craft spaces that authentically reflect and serve their communities. Raised in cities across India, Koa was shaped by the intersection of many marginalized identities, embracing the beauty of being queer—a perpetual outsider, even among outsiders. In this periphery, however, they find a profound richness: a deep well of spirituality, kinship, and creativity. Beyond their work in real estate, Koa serves on the board of Family Tree Clinic, a super-rad sexual and reproductive justice org. They ground themselves in writing and movement-based practices like butoh and qigong while exploring the world of watercolor. For Koa, art-making is both a healing modality and an invitation. To play, to be, and to belong.

Mankwe Ndosi is a Song Catcher and Culture Worker based in Minneapolis. She is a member of the Association for the Advancement of Creative Musicians (AACM Chicago/ New York), and a Resident Community Engaged Artist at Pillsbury House and Theatre. She is a lay herbalist and a Wise Woman ever growing in her practice of listening to and learning with the plant world. Mankwe is a commitment to emergent engagements of earth, sound, and regeneration through creative and embodied practices.

Lela Pierce is a Black Multiracial visual artist and dancer born in rural MniSota Makoce. She grew up playing in prairies, forests and waterfalls while communing with horses, goats, chickens, frogs and birds. Lela has danced extensively with Ananya Dance Theater, Rosy Simas Danse and Pramila Vasudevan. She teaches Sculpture at Macalester College. In 2018 she received the Jerome Emerging Artist Fellowship for visual art and at this time she is a current Jerome Hill Fellowship artist.

Pramila Vasudevan is of Tamil descent, and is a Twin-Cities-based movement-centered artist, culture worker, and maker of community-rooted/routed transdisciplinary work. She has been living and working on Dakota land, Mni Sota Makoce since 1995. Vasudevan is the founder and artistic director of Aniccha Arts (2004–2024), an arts collaborative producing site-specific performances that examine agency, voice, and group dynamics within community histories, institutions, and systems. She is an artist associate of Pillsbury House Theatre. She has been honored with Mcknight (2024, 2016), Joyce Award (2022), United States Artists (2022) and Guggenheim (2017) fellowships in choreography. Her current practice involves gardening, hosting conversations and gatherings, and developing improvisational movement sessions inspired by growing practices in gardens and greenhouses and by plant cycles in urban areas.

Jeffrey Wells (he/him) is queer performance creator, performer, designer, technician, and administrator working in Minneapolis for the past 18 years. He is a co-founder and current member of the performance ensemble SuperGroup, which has been creating all kinds of performance experiences for most of that time. He currently spends his time exploring and cultivating novelty and non-habitual behavior through his Feldenkrais practice as well as supporting artistic endeavors in his beloved Twin Cities' weirdo performance community, including projects with Rosy Simas and Emily Gastineau. Past collaborations include works by WaxFactory/Rachel Jendrzejewski, Valerie Oliveiro, Eric Larson/Toot Performance, Kaz Sherman, Fire Drill, Mad King Thomas, Judith Howard among others.

Freedom Is Fundamental

S. M. Foysol Ahmed, Heather Cleary, and Gwendolyn Hooks

These poems were created as part of a time-limited community empathy writing project that looked to Zora Neale Hurston and Langston Hughes as writers to inspire creative writing conversations about the importance of friendship to social mobility. Seventeen writers were actively involved, which included seven college students (medicine, counselor education, and social work), one faculty member, six high school students, and three community members who joined together for five months. From November 2023 to March 2024, these writers wrote in response to three prompts a month. An example of a prompt shared as a writing community is a quote from ZNH, "There are years that ask questions and years that answer." Each writer in the writing community took no more than 10 minutes to write independently about the quote (fiction, poetry, essay). Then, without censoring, they shared their writing in a shared document, online video, or in a virtual or in-person writing group. This collaborative sharing inspired and challenged each writer to think critically and to stretch creatively. Three writers from the writing community volunteered to be a part of the data analysis process after the writing community had completed all fifteen writing prompts. After reading through all the community's writing, several themes emerged for this smaller analysis team. Each of the three writers who were part of the analysis picked one of their poems from the process that they felt best represented three of the discovered themes: freedom is fundamental to personal fulfillment, dreams are important but hard work, and life is uncertain.

We acknowledge that this unique writing process was a community effort and that little glints of every writer involved in the project can be seen in the three poems selected. We would like to take this opportunity to acknowledge the other writers involved in the community empathy write: Tina Debord, Chantal Crane, Tamara Peacock, Ayanna Jordan, Kylah Griffin, Busi Nkosi, Talacia Coleman, Daire'yon Watson, Anna Stuchel, Haider Alhajri, Sydnee Savage-Utley, Lukas Hardy, Javion Finn, and MacArthur Johnson.

S. M. Foysol Ahmed

In the Silence

Inspired by Langston Hughes' "Dreams"

In the silence of ruins, dreams whisper still.
A child with eyes wide, in the night's chill.
War's shadow looms, yet hope dares to gleam.
Amidst the rubble, a fragile dream.

"A broken-winged bird," the child stands alone.
Yet clings to visions of a peaceful home.
Lost laughter, lost love, in memory's keep.
Fueling the dreams that disturb the sleep.

Through tear-streaked gaze, stars seem to say.
Hold fast to dreams, they'll light your way.

Heather M. Sloane Cleary

The Assumption

Inspired by Langston Hughes' "Freedom"

"Let things take their course"
Is a poison of sorts
This phrase sounds so reasonable
And demands very little it seems

The assumption is that the course will lead to freedom
But this has never been the case

To sit quiet hoping for change is intuitively too easy
Deep down we know change is a fight

A fight of words
A fight to be heard
A fight to be acknowledged
A fight to not be silenced, to not be made invisible

Tomorrow is another day
A day to push up against what is wrong
Maybe today only an inch
Another day a mile
And some days we will feel defeated and exhausted

Tomorrow is another day
Don't waste it waiting
On oppression to strengthen.

Gwendolyn Hooks

Answers

Inspired by Zora Neale Hurston's line in *Their Eyes Are Watching God*: "There are years that ask questions and years that answer."

Answers: we all want answers to life's questions. These answers never seem to come in the time we want them to; there is almost always a delay. Think Spring, we eagerly await Spring after a long brutal Michigan winter, but still in April, the crisp air of winter remains. What if we could choose when the answers would come and the exact questions we wish to answer. We could fashion ourselves as soothsayers with the ability to predict and maybe predetermine a direction based on knowing the answer.

I suppose though, there are those questions to which there are no answers. Those questions that linger in the back of all our minds, things like, why is there so much human suffering? Who determines who thrives and who does not? Even, what is the purpose of life? These are questions we all yearn to have answers to without realizing what it would truly mean to know.

Knowing can be a powerful thing, and power is good, right? What might we do with this knowledge and how might it change our lives, or what we know or believe to be? I imagine often what it might be like to have knowledge of all things, to have no unanswered questions. Would that be enough? Enough to fulfill my need to know and gain some level of power in such knowing. What is it that I really seek?

Authors Bios

S M Foysol Ahmed is a Social Work PhD student and Research Assistant at the University of Kentucky College of Social Work. Foysol participated in the Community Empathy Writing program as an international participant from Bangladesh. He is an experienced international social worker and researcher, holding a Master of Social Work degree from the University of Toledo and a bachelor's in health economics degree from the University of Dhaka (Bangladesh). With over six years of expertise in macro-level social work, his work experience spans diverse fields, including mental health, human trafficking prevention, labor rights advocacy, and advocating for climate and environmental justice.

Heather M Sloane Cleary teaches social work at the University of Toledo and runs a creative writing social justice group called Fearless Writers. This work was from the second of three community empathy writes that blend creative writing with public health considerations. Writing with others is her way to bring people separated by the injustice of redlining together in hopes of raising awareness about the implicit bias that is created by the distances between us.

Gwendolyn Hooks is a doctoral candidate in counselor education at the University of Toledo. She has a passion for people and language, both of which have inspired her career as a mental health counselor. Writing, especially creative writing, on purpose with a purpose is a way to momentarily step out of academia, a place where community, empathy, and awareness of others are often strangers. Writing in this space has been an opportunity to see people and become more aware of myself in relation to others and [re]connect with the ancient Zulu principle of "*I am because we are.*"

The Sound You Never Forget

Ania Payne

Reflection

Even though I've been teaching community writing projects in my Professional Writing courses for the past six years, each semester brings surprising learning moments, realizations, and new characters into the classroom. No two community writing projects are ever the same, even when working with the same organization over multiple semesters. Over the course of a six-year partnership with Habitat, for example, the classes have moved from creating promotional content about Habitat's programs, to collaboratively writing Habitat Homeowner profile articles, to helping the staff at Habitat develop a writing culture within their workplace. Since this long-term relationship has deepened, Habitat now trusts my students to work with the beneficiaries of their services – the homeowners – which is a much more closely entwined collaboration than having students revise and update their brochures. Last semester, students traveled all around the county to sit down, interview, and collaboratively write and edit these articles with Habitat's homeowners. That particular project isn't included in this essay because this series of vignettes only captures snapshots of my first semester incorporating community writing projects into my Professional Writing classroom. But this piece aims to highlight how community writing adds a unique sense of life and personality to a course, even when projects don't go exactly as planned.

The Sound You Never Forget

"When I was a student in this classroom thirty years ago, the professor used to smoke cigarettes while delivering lectures!" Frank leans back in the desk, which seems toy-sized for his large frame. He props his feet on another desk and yawns loudly. The director of our local Habitat for Humanity affiliate hadn't told me that she was bringing her husband to class, yet here they both are in the dank basement classroom of the humanities building.

My students, mostly business majors whose classes primarily occur in our new multi-million dollar business building, look both alarmed and amused. A few of them shift uncomfortably in stiff, wrinkled suits that a finance professor requires them to wear on Wednesdays. I notice some students slyly recording Snapchat videos of Frank, but he seems unaware, which is surprising only because he had just told us about his private detective business, "Silver Eagle Investigations, LLC."

Once Melody gets her slideshow pulled up, she starts to talk about the work that Habitat for Humanity does in our community and the projects that the students will be creating for our community writing project. They listen to her keenly, probably relieved to have a break from hearing me lecture at them about the importance of using the "you attitude" in business writing, or how to format a report or write a persuasive proposal. As Melody delivers her presentation, the students ask questions about how the community typically responds to Habitat's work and messaging, and they seem excited that their writing could make an impact in the community. The students start chiming in with ideas about how Habitat could share their projects on social media or post flyers around the ReStore for customers who aren't as tech-savvy. It's obvious that this project is already engaging them more than writing another hypothetical memo to Michael Scott.

While Melody answers the students' questions, Frank drifts off to sleep. He's probably heard Melody's spiel before. He never really explains why he's here, and I don't ask. Melody nudges him awake at the end of the class and before she leaves, the students and I thank her for joining us and for letting us work on writing projects with Habitat this semester.

~

In the next class period, another section of Professional Writing students is partnering with our local animal shelter. The director, Willie, is in class, along with Princess, an adoptable mutt who's been living at the shelter. Princess is the size of a Chihuahua but has long, wiry hair and manic blue eyes that dart anxiously around the room. Willie doesn't have a slideshow and he wants us to sit in a large circle, so we rearrange the chairs.

"Students, do you know why you need to get your pets neutered and spayed?" he asks, pushing his dark hair away from his eyes. Princess lets out a low whine. This group of students is quieter than the morning class, and they look at Willie nervously, wearing similar expressions as Princess.

"Because left to their own devices, they'll bang anything that moves and overpopulate the earth! I heard a German Shepherd with a Golden Retriever in heat the other week, and let me tell you, that's a sound you never forget." Willie purses his lips and lets out a high-pitched, feral moan, forcing eye contact with each student as he makes sounds that have probably never been made in this building before. I silently hope that my Department Head doesn't walk down the hallway.

As Willie talks, some of the students jot down notes in their notebooks, though I'm not sure about what—the sounds of mating dogs, or the romance between a German Shepherd and a Golden Retriever, maybe. None of these topics are directly related to our project that is supposed to help spread literacy about animal health for the shelter, or maybe they are. Since I'm letting Willie take the lead on deciding what the students write, maybe these mating intonations *will* be useful for their brochures.

It's my first semester partnering with community organizations, and I'm learning to release control, something that doesn't come naturally to type-A instructors like myself. Although I usually have the semester's projects planned months in advance, I quickly realize that this level of planning is impossible when I'm bringing community partners into the classroom. The 16-week semester timeline means as little to them as syllabus policies about sleeping during lectures or bringing animals into campus buildings (since Princess isn't a service dog, she's not technically allowed to be with us right now). By ignoring the manufactured rigidity of the academy, these community partners reinvigorate the classroom. We're no longer going through the same routine of lectures and think-pair-shares; instead, we're spontaneous, not sure what will be said or how we'll react. Nobody's eyes are glued to the clock.

Princess disappears behind a pile of backpacks, and after a moment a student raises her hand to say, "Um, Willie? Princess just peed on the floor."

~

In the third class of the day, another community partner with a doctorate from Harvard uses words that are probably beyond half of the students' comprehension. Reba delivers a lecture about the state of our community's health and wellbeing. She pushes students to fight for equity through personal commitments and by arguing for policy, system, and environmental reforms. She explains how the infographics that students are creating for this project will help the nonprofit increase health literacy in the community, since the students will translate complex topics about nutrition into image and narrative-driven infographics. Reba tells stories about food deserts in our community and neighborhoods that are cut off from our public transportation system, and students look shocked to learn about the inequality that exists right outside of our campus walls.

When one student asks, "Well, if they aren't happy in that neighborhood, can't they just move?" Reba is quick to respond.

"Do you remember when you moved into your dorm? Did your parents help you pack up and move in?"

The student nods.

"Right, and you probably had to pay a security deposit, and maybe some other fees in addition to the rent?"

The student nods again.

"And if you have a lot of furniture that you're moving, and no truck, there's another cost for the U-Haul. All of these fees add up and make it very difficult to *just move*. And that's assuming that people can get out of their leases, and that they're able to move on days that they're not working, and that they have enough friends or family willing to help them move."

The student nods and doesn't look offended or ready to argue. He just leans back in his desk, contemplatively.

~

In the following weeks, some students become so invested that they start volunteering at the Habitat for Humanity ReStore or the county animal shelter, and they tell me about how restorative it is to have these meaningful community connections. Melody (but not Frank) and Reba even return during the last week of class to watch the students deliver their final projects. Willie, however, quits his job as the director of the animal shelter two weeks before the end of the semester, which I only learn about when his administrative assistant responds to one of my frantic emails asking for his feedback on the students' drafts.

In this moment of unexpected turnover, nobody else at the animal shelter has the capacity to take over Willie's role in our class project, but the shelter reassures us that they still want the students' brochures at the end of the semester. I spend a day panicking about how we'll move forward without Willie's involvement. But eventually, I realize that this is completely out of my control, and that even though we've lost our point of contact at the shelter, the project must adjust and go on.

During the last week of the semester, students email their brochures to the animal shelter and receive brief "Thank you!" emails from Willie's assistant. While my other classes got detailed revision suggestions from their community partners before they submitted their final drafts, Princess's new friends and I had to work through the uncertainty together, which prompted us to discuss what happens when someone you've been collaborating with abruptly quits a project. During our final class period together, we reflect on our partnership with the animal shelter. I try not to come across as being too disappointed, but I let them know that I was hoping the shelter's staff would have been more involved with the project so that it could have been a reciprocal partnership; I don't mention this, but I know that the shelter would be more likely to use the students' documents if they had offered some revision suggestions for their drafts. However, the students don't seem as troubled by Willie's abrupt departure, and as they pack up their bags to leave the class one final time, they express hopes that Willie is doing well, wherever he is, and that Princess has finally found a home.

Author Bio

Ania Payne, PhD, is an Assistant Professor of Writing at Kansas State University. Ania's scholarly agenda focuses on asset-based approaches to community writing partnerships in the English courses that she teaches. She also develops community writing programs with nonprofit partners and examines community storytelling as a mode of inquiry.

Two Poems by Three Authors

Bonnie Vidrine-Isbell, Aurora Matzke, and Genesea Carter

Reflection

The three of us, though at three different universities, have been writing academic pieces together since 2017, after we were all on a *CCCC* panel together about how systems influence WPA work. We began to collaborate together when we realized we had shared experiences as WPAs working in similar-but-different complex systems–systems that, at times, constricted us. Realizing three voices are stronger together than one, our collaborations have allowed us to open up and be vulnerable in ways we could not or should not be on our own.

All of our collaborations begin with a text thread about what is going on in our lives. Usually, one of us shares a sticky problem at work. We then create Zoom conversations to talk about what is shaping and affecting us. As we talk, we often muse on what resonates or departs from our experiences across institutions. The time to just be allows us to be vulnerable and safe–and also facilitates brainstorming about potential topics, theoretical bents, and examples we might include if we were to share our thoughts further. If we think we have a kernel of an idea, the writing process often begins as a mosaic of tile pieces–we take different sections to start drafting but allow ourselves to write over and across each other, as we are drawn to.

The first poem comes from conversations we have had about assemblages–how our three different theoretical influences (Genesea: systems theory; Aurora: feminist theory; Bonnie: neuroscience) and administrative experiences intersect and constellate into a third voice, a collective voice. Our third voice allows us to tend to ourselves and each other, speaking and writing when it feels untenable to speak in our singular voices. A third voice also cultivates cognitive play, where our brain development and personal growth depend upon co-thinking/co-challenging interactions that build new neural networks and recalibrate embodiment. Understanding ourselves as embodied beings in a post-human world helps to center our conversations around ourselves, our communities, and the systems in which we find ourselves in productive ways–intentionally working toward identifying where action and reaction are taking place, while also making room for layers of emotion to coexist, such as celebration, excitement, mourning, sadness, and joy. So, for this poem we challenged ourselves to each create a metaphor for connection to follow this concept of assemblages. For example, Genesea uses the metaphor of pieces of shells longing to be reunited amidst the systems and rules that separate us (laws of nature in the case of the shell).

In the second poem, we wrote a villanelle about the process of belonging, with each stanza representing a step in the process of becoming part of a community. A villanelle is a strict form of poetry that aims to increase in magnitude of emotion/experience as it proceeds; we encourage readers to learn more about the form, if they are curious. We chose this structure because it allows us to collaboratively Kintsugi: playing with the Japanese art form of "fixing" pottery cracks with gold as a verb, the villanelle encouraged us to write in a way that filled our own emotional and experiential "cracks" with the gold from our friendship, our encouragement, and our collaborations. Each stanza of our poem takes on a different aspect of belonging that is necessary for a group connection, moving from initial connection to having the group know your name to feeling known and befriended.

Finally, as part of our writing process, we asked our friend and poet, Christopher Davidson, to give us feedback. This is not an uncommon step when we write together. There are usually several friends, colleagues, and neighbors who rhyzomatically slide in and out of our writing. He collaborated with us and helped with editing and proofreading.

Our goal was just this–to write together about community and belonging, and to have fun together with words and language.

Assemblages

A moment of silence. My fingers gently brush
the soft lines of sand, shells, driftwood all crushed
in millions of pieces, connected but apart,
falling softly through my hand, longing for their counterpart.

A breeze whispers in my ear as it gently moves past
calling for our meaning and connection to last.
The systems and rules, bones and sinews, make us long for more,
separated like millions of pieces alone on the shore.

Sunlight through the prism, language through the soul—
Colors in words and identities flood a kitchen wall.
Our hands chase rainbows like meanings we don't know.
We cannot grasp what others say unless we grow.

Warm, yellow kitchen–words all around–
Will I quiet the mind and listen—sit myself down?
Even seeing in color, understanding is hard work.
Making friends is fieldwork.

I pull the lid from the white, plastic paint bucket, the smell
of rot thick in the air. Rind, the shell
of some forgotten bird, and heat
breaks down creation, like shallow peat.

My hands reach into the bucket, its decomposing earth
Possibilities in my palm. I measure its worth.
My trowel turns the soil gently, years of death, of worth
All used, none forgotten, fingerprints in new birth.

To Belong

You must not only go; you must stay[1]
And be *part of,* with intent—
Eye to eye, our faces on display.

Converted light, electrical impulse, stardust ray
Pulled, a part of sinew and bone, all bent
Energy caught and gone; you must stay

My feelings that, like broken teacups, mosaiced, lay
Where soul directs in descent
Words through my eyes, feelings on display.

In each step, in each toe, I feel the earth today.
The warm grit of dirt is loose, resistant,
Is fractal: You must go, you must stay.

My jaw aches to be heard in what you say.
I dump my tea on you, and you catch its unspent
Language. My eyes to your eyes, our faces on display,

Like bells before an open doorway.
We walk in–connected, known, present
To each other. Why go? I'd rather stay.
Two eyes to two eyes, our meaning on display.

---

1. Christopher Davidson, editor and fellow collaborator

Author Bios

Bonnie Vidrine-Isbell is an Associate Professor of English. She teaches language, rhetoric, and writing. Her research blends bilingual brain studies and second language pedagogy. She has taught English as a second and foreign language in Washington, Louisiana, Thailand, Spain, Belize, and now California. She also built and currently directs the English Language Scholars at Biola, which provides academic language support to students. Bonnie's scholarly work appears in academic collections such as *Contemporary Perspectives on Cognition and Writing* and *Translingual Pedagogical Perspectives*.

Aurora Matzke is an Assistant Professor in the English & Modern Languages Department at Cal Poly, Pomona. She enjoys learning about and working toward ways to create successful access pathways for all students. Most recently, she collaboratively guest edited a special issue of *Peitho* based on feminist coalition building and authored a chapter in *Mentorship and Methodology*. In press are a collaboratively written article in a *College English* special issue devoted to consent and a chapter in *Bad Ideas About Writing and AI*.

Genesea M. Carter is Associate Director of Composition and Associate Professor of Rhetoric and Composition at Colorado State University. Her work has appeared in *Composition Studies, Journal of Teaching Writing, Open Words: Access and English Studies,* and *Writers: Craft and Context*. She has guest edited *Academic Labor: Research and Artistry* and co-edited *Class in the Composition Classroom: Pedagogy and the Working Class* and *Systems Shift: Creating and Navigating Change in Rhetoric and Composition Program Administration*.

#WeAllWrite/We All Right

Tabitha Espina and Kelvin Keown

Visual Project Personal Reflections

As a collaborative activity between the Director of Writing and Writing Center staff, we provide two reflections on the process of creating this visual project.

Tabitha

As the new Director of Writing at an Asian American and Native American Pacific-Islander-Serving Institution, I wanted to learn more about the literacies that run (through) our campus. When the National Council of Teachers of English (NCTE) promoted the National Day on Writing on October 20, I thought that maybe a week-long activity at the Writing Center would be an opportunity to, according to the NCTE, "[celebrate] writing—and the many places, reasons, and ways we write each day—as an essential component of literacy," thus fostering a sense of community as writers using our own languages together, for a variety of purposes. Perhaps I had even hoped that the activity would creatively confront the common critique of "Why can't students write?" with a resounding "Yes, #WeAllWrite! (phonetically "We all right!")," affirming the value of multiple languages and literacies at play.

Kelvin

As a staff member in the writing center, I was excited to host this ongoing activity, because we take every opportunity to assure students that we are all writers and that no one is born a "good" writer. Furthermore, I work to encourage the stance that we are all language learners all the time, and that writing is so much more than a sum of a list of rules (grammatical, conventional). We hoped that a low-stakes activity like this that approaches writing from a place of humility, commonality, and accessibility can encourage participants' perception of themselves as writers, worthy and capable of academic writing.

The Prompt and Process

We asked anyone on campus and part of the campus community to write, on a sticky note, either the last 10 words they had recently written or about the last thing they had written. Some responses were featured on social media with the hashtags #WeAllWrite or #WhyIWrite. Collecting these responses gave us insight into the richness of the literate lives of our students, faculty, staff, and visitors to our campus. Responses displayed a multitude of forms through which ideas take shape. When we transcribed each of the responses, we preserved as many of the original details as possible to show how each writer was indulging in the capacities of their languages to enrich their inner lives or relate with others. This artwork, then, attempts to convey this juxtapositioning of forms, shapes, languages, and purposes—rearranged and grouped together. When read aloud for lyricism and coherence, these are the sounds of #WeAllWrite. A visual poetry generator "wrote" the #WeAllWrite hashtag with these responses. We encouraged student employees (writing tutors, study habit support mentors, receptionists) to contribute their own sticky notes so that the activity was sufficiently modeled for students, staff, and faculty passing by. Writing Center receptionists, furthermore, attended to the board and encouraged participation. Participants often asked for clarification about the activity (i.e., "What is this?") or picked up their phones, possibly to read a recent text message to write on a sticky note. In these ways, our own composing processes were shared in community to portray community creatively. We hope to continue this work in the years to come, especially in these tumultuous times in education, to show that together "we all write" to be alright.

"I write for a lot of reasons! documenting my favorite moments in journals 🖤📓."
I 🖤📊 STATISTICS (which requires a lot of writing.) communicating with friends #whywewrite"
"I am at a writing conference in Tacoma, WA. Yay!"
"Because I think I'm right #whyIwrite"
"C U shortly I guess I see everyone shortly LOL #WeAllWrite"
"Megan Thee Stallion's new release is my ** vibe! 😎"
"#WhyIWrite In order to understand myself"
"I'll let you know again when I plan on going again"
"Because Zeth is never right teehee #whyIwrite"

"It's me Hi"
"I write for various reason but what I love the most in writing is to express my feelings, emotions, and my story #WhyIWrite"
"...Agreed definitely that nothing major is needed, still reading though..."
"Organizational ante narratives, institutional narrative ecologies, HE leadership"
"#WeAllWrite Come meet your peer success mentors! Mingle and learn what they do over free pumpkin spice coffee"
"We're teaching 9 to 5 the Dolly Parton movie! #Weallwrite"
"#WeAllWrite YOU should definitely visit Tokyo and Kyoto someday"
"Hey, YSauce Brazil here"

```
"You're on the right track girl, I got your back girl!"
"#WhyIwrite It makes me happy ☺"
"Check comments on the post, the artist is so
nice #WeAllWrite"
"I write to get everything out of my mind. I'm
a chatter-box"
"Not sure ☺"
"I write to represent myself and what I stand
for #WhyIWrite"
"#WhyIWrite I have funny & clever things I need to share
☺ "
"I write to make sense of the world and my thoughts"
"#WhyIWrite I write to clear my head and ease my mind 🖤"
"Linguistic identity bi-dialectical multilingual, slang,
profanity, digital I feel speak accommodation"
"I write because I love creating stories and tell-
ing them"
"I write to put the things in my brain into a physical
form. I write to organize my thoughts into words. Cram-
```

ing abstracts and complex emotions into the confine of the english language. It helps me understand myself"
"Think there's more than one implied listener in the song"
"I'm almost 48 for accurate math. Did you get jeans?"

"I may have been hungry when I put together the box"
"#WeallWrite Does it really make him a better, more well-rounded character?"
"- Chalakiles - -green salsa –chips (tortilla) -crema (sour cream) -Queso cotija –chicken"
"#WeAllWrite She had especially never seen a male in the neighborhood before 😊"
"...quickly grew in strength in the early months of 1776. (from a slide deck)"
"#WhyIWrite Sometimes shows are inspiring but I don't like when they end so fanfics are necessary"
"Be a John Wick"
"I can try looking up slightly less intensive recipes"
"The sheet music The judge's form is the music"
"A is represented by the consonants. W is a vector."
"Do you like glue sticks???? Enter date of ascension of this dog. 🐶 "ribbit""
"May the valkyries welcome you and lead you through Odin's great battlefield. May they sing your name with love & joy, so that we might hear it rise from the depths of Volholk and knew you've taken your rightful place at Hitabulkies"

Author Bios

Tabitha Espina is Director of Writing and Assistant Professor of Writing Studies at the University Washington Tacoma. She is a third-generation Filipina born and raised in Guåhan. She has published in *College English, Race and Pedagogy Journal, Asian Studies, Humanities Diliman, Okinawan Journal of Island Studies, Pacific Asia Inquiry,* and *Micronesian Educator,* as well as in collections from the Modern Language Association and University of Pittsburgh Press. Her research interests include decolonial theories and pedagogies, transpacific rhetorics, and island feminisms.

Kelvin Keown is the English Learner Specialist at the University of Washington Tacoma Writing Center. He has taught and tutored in higher education for 20 years and holds a Masters in Teaching English to Speakers of Other Languages. His professional interests include sociolinguistics, tutor training, and tutoring multilingual writers.

The Pond

Joonna Smitherman Trapp

Personal Reflection

I am a professor of Writing and Rhetoric. I was asked to direct a regional retreat for Christian women at an encampment off in the Georgia hills. As primarily a teacher of college students, I had to plan how to teach these women of all ages and educational backgrounds who desired to spend the retreat integrating their faith (the common thread and value among them) with social justice issues, especially women's issues. I adapted the traditional rhetorical triangle (exigency, audience, constraints) to aid in my workshop development and planning.

Participants' Personal Experience/Faith

Exigency in Social Justice Issues   Constraints (Writing/Communication & 3 days)

How might I be able to bring what I knew about writing's power to change or enhance perspectives and realign value systems during this retreat? For the three days of the retreat, I engaged the women in meditative practices, discussions, careful and safe voluntary sharing, writing, speaking, and thinking beyond themselves about the world and the role of people of faith in societal change. I used for exemplars women leaders from the Bible, as well as Christian advocates for change in American history such as abolitionist Angelina Grimké. For the final day, I led a three-hour *lectio divina* which centered on a shared text(s). *Lectio divina* or "divine reading" is an ancient method (Jewish and Christian) of making a text alive and understood at a deep level. In the workshop we read our selected text orally twice while in a circle, all participating in the reading. After some quiet and meditation, participants spontaneously read phrases or words into the circle. We continued this until there was silence. The words of our text were illuminated by the impromptu ordering and sequencing. New meanings of the text were created.

After listening, speaking, repeating, and reflection, all offered impromptu, I sent the participants away from the little community we had formed over the three days for a solid hour of writing. No talking. What came out of that experience was remarkable–a meaningful shared documentation of a community thinking together about faith and social justice. We set personal goals as we exited the retreat. We also set goals for how we might influence our own faith communities to care, learn, and do more in the areas around us.

The retreat impacted me as well. During that hour of sustained writing, I sat beside the lovely little pond in the hills and began a description exercise. Beyond the beauty of the pond, I began to see more about the pond, the complications and natural evolution of the pond's maturing process. The pond began to become an image for me of much of what we had been talking about during the retreat: the difficulties of seeing things from positions of privilege, looking past what is obvious to what might lay hidden, recent conversations in the media about human trafficking and how our purchasing patterns perpetuate those evil systems, the victimization of women—all key topics during the retreat. We all shared our writing upon reuniting. This poem that came out of me that day seemed for all of us to summarize our work together during the retreat and set our thoughts and plans for work in our respective faith communities.

I have since heard from some of these women that they have begun conversations in their faith communities about being more active in social justice work and in leadership roles. Some also report that writing and goal setting has become a bigger part of their faith and community work.

The Pond

The world is like this pond
    here
in the wide green meadow
ripples so gentle the trees stand uninterrupted
watery clouds lounge silently behind
serene
    until suddenly
gaping mouth from the depths hits the surface
a dragonfly with iridescent wings
    disappears
gone into the dark
little hope for
spread of wing again
    abducted.

The world is like this pond
    here
at midday in the half light of cloudy sky
seeming tranquil peaceful but
with a light foul order from unseen bottom sludge
hidden hunger below the surface
    survival
of the fittest played out
exactly the kind of world which ought to have
    disappeared
two thousand years ago.

The world is like this pond
    luring
our daughters with promises of love and beauty
when it swallows them whole in one gulp
all we see is graceful meadow and
    con artist trees.

How many daughters will slip quietly
    unnoticed
into this treacherous pond
consumed by the maws of abuse and suffering?

How many before we treat the pond's water
    with hope, service, and love,
adding the beneficial organism of ourselves which

dissipates the sticky sludge unseen underneath?

Then the world's ponds will shimmer
    clear to the bottom
our daughters suddenly free
will swim in sweet water without fear

And God will clap hands in
    delight.
                    ~Joonna Smitherman Trapp

Author Bio

Joonna Smitherman Trapp is recently retired from Emory University where she served as the Director of the Emory Writing Program and Writing Across Emory for several years. She has also served as a department chair at two small colleges earlier in her professional life and taught a wide range of courses in the areas of composition, rhetoric, and literature. In retirement, she is eagerly finding time for her writing life again. Currently living in a national forest on her family's farmland, she is doing elder care for her father. During these "in-between-years," poetry provides a welcome repose and teacher for meditative writerly practices.

the intersection: Balance of a Wait-less World

The Moonlight Cheese Alliance and Leslee N. Johnson

> "How to be a human being?
> First, learn how to fall.
> Second, learn to live in pain.
> Third, learn to get lost and find your way again."
> –Shunyu Huang, from "How to…," *the intersection*, Fall 2024

> "Do we all reflect stars?
> The Universe joins our season."
> –Enjoy33 from "Relief…," *the intersection*, Fall 2024

The intersection of State Street and Haywood Road in West Asheville bears witness to heavy traffic every day of the week. In the heart of a gentrified neighborhood, and the main gateway to Asheville's largest public housing community and homeless encampment, the intersection is a crossing of disparate paths. This corner is the home of 12 Baskets Cafe and Community Center.

12 Baskets Cafe offers free, hot, sit-down meals and free grocery shopping six days a week, serving high quality food rescued from Asheville's wealth of restaurants and boutique grocery stores. Without distinction between those serving and those served, we all wait tables, wash dishes, and break bread at round tables decked out in bright mismatched tablecloths. We greet each other by name and recognize one another as a human among humans, no matter what.

> "the people that populate this quirky garden of Eden . . ."
> –Jorge, from "write yourself into the future…" *the intersection*, Fall 2024

Every Friday, the writer's collective, the Moonlight Cheese Alliance, gathers under a maple tree. We hand out notebooks and pens and write on a shared prompt for 10-15 minutes. Then we listen to each other's wide and wild variations on the same theme that take the form of poems, scenes and stories. We don't take ourselves too seriously, but we do take our words seriously enough to listen closely and pay attention.

On September 27, 2024, Hurricane Helene devastated the city of Asheville. The banks of the French Broad, which offered sites for parking or setting up camp in an overdeveloped city, were razed under 24 feet of water. We still don't know how many lives were lost. At 12 Baskets Cafe, folks made sandwiches in the dark for days. The writing collective continued to meet every Friday, as regulars and new participants showed up or stumbled in. We didn't write on prompts about floods, or destruction, aftermath, loss or grief. Those themes and images of water, darkness, wind and wreckage came up naturally, embedded in narratives and poems that also reached towards hope, sanity, and a post-apocalyptic vision of a world that can't ignore everything that goes wrong.

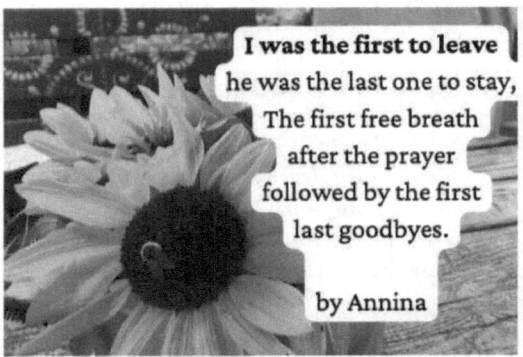

I was the first to leave
he was the last one to stay,
The first free breath
after the prayer
followed by the first
last goodbyes.

by Annina

Milk, cigarettes
this day in the past
filling up my gas can.
Vape $$
paying my bills
taking my pills
getting on the bus
walking & running
Hustler
Worker
Gang life
God's life
My life

by Brandon

> *"the sea has risen to meet us where we are*
> *we hold our breath*
> *and submerge ourselves*
> *a communal baptism*
> *a new way of seeing*
> *under water."*
> –Atlas, from "Imagine this…" *the intersection,* Fall 2024

We've been writing together for almost three years, and in that time, have accumulated a large body of work, which we are called to share in print with a larger audience. Using funds donated at a handful of public readings, we've published quarterly zines since the Spring of 2024. The Fall 2024 edition of *the intersection* was published in late October 2024 and contains work created both before the flood and after. The work appears largely unedited except for small changes for clarity. We believe it is important to make our experiences and poetry legible in a world where we often find ourselves and our lives illegible, so we type everyone's pieces in a shared document. But we also wanted to use the graphic design of the zine to convey the immediacy of the writing, so we included hand-drawn artwork and superimposed typed pieces over images of the handwritten pages.

> *"We're alright.*
> *On the pier, we are playing*
> *hop-scotch and rummy*
> *and learning how to braid each other's hair*
> *and pick our noses discreetly."*
> –Robin, from "the ferryman…" *the intersection,* Fall 2024

It is with grace, humor, a shared longing for belonging, and to be seen and heard, that the writers of the Moonlight Cheese Alliance offer the third edition of our zine *the intersection*: *Balance of a Wait-Less World*. To access the zine, please scan the QR code.

Author Bios

ACE, Amori, Annina, Atlas, Brandon, Brian, Brooke, Collin, Cormac, Daniel B., Donovan, Drew, Elliot, Enjoy33, Greg, Hays, Hazel, Jackson, Jasmine Mae, Jody, Kitty, Kristina, Leslee, Liam, Luke, Mae, Margaret, Melenn, Nathan, Oliver, Paul M., Robin, Ryan, Shaad, Shunyu, Silvia, Susan and Zariyah are writers of the Moonlight Cheese Alliance. We are artists, filmmakers, activists, students, musicians, educators, wizards, creators, interfaith and intergenerational. Our work and daily lives take us to all corners of Asheville, from the anarchist bookstore, to UNC Asheville, to busking hotspots downtown. We come together every Friday in the garden at 12 Baskets Cafe. Some of us stay for an afternoon, or a season before moving on, some of us have been writing together for three years.

Leslee N. Johnson is a writer and educator living in Western North Carolina, with an academic background in philosophy and creative writing. As a lecturer at UNC Asheville, she teaches humanities, first-year writing and professional writing, taking her classes into the city of Asheville through community engaged coursework. She co-facilitates the writing collective, Moonlight Cheese Alliance, at Asheville Poverty Initiative's 12 Baskets Cafe in West Asheville, which gives her space to practice her own poetry. Since 2022, she has served as the Director of UNC Asheville's Prison Education Program, with the opportunity to teach inside, and work with state and county entities to design and support college-credit bearing programs that address the needs of students impacted by the justice system and poverty.

How We See Free

Debbie Allen, Susann Moeller, Chuck Salmons, Rikki Santer, and Karen Scott

Reflection

Throughout 2024, the Ohio Poetry Association and Poets Against Racism & Hate USA (organizations for which we serve as leaders) presented the Ohio Underground Railroad Whistle-Stop Poetry Tour. This series of events honored Ohio's role in the Underground Railroad and raised awareness of issues of social injustice, hate, and prejudice past and present. At historically important sites such as homes that were Underground Railroad stations and a church founded on abolitionist principles, the tour's poets enlightened and inspired audiences. They read and performed works of witness by historic poets and their own poems conceived from lived experiences and intense interest in allyship.

The events included poetry readings and workshops, history talks, musical and interpretive performances, walking tours, and other programming. Central to the tour was a traveling collaborative writing project. At each tour stop, attendees—adults and children alike—responded in writing to the question "What does freedom mean to you?" This endeavor helped participants tap their feelings and thoughts about the subject matter, and the group writing experience created a sense of communal belonging. Event attendees walked away pledging to "be more aware," "gain more knowledge," and "speak out more" about social justice issues. As well, they left behind pieces of themselves that would be assembled into a multivoiced view of freedom. The poem "How We See Free" emerged from the more than 100 responses to our question.

We composed "How We See Free" as a contrapuntal comprising three poems in vertical columns that form a fourth poem when read horizontally. In developing the poem, we compiled and arranged participants' responses using their exact words. To achieve effective flow and other artistic qualities, we made minor adjustments to verb tense, pronouns, and so forth and separated or slightly rearranged parts of certain entries. After its creation, the poem was formatted and printed as an 11 × 17-inch broadside [shown on next page]. We chose the contrapuntal form because it allowed for the meaningful juxtaposition of the many contributions to the poem's development. Furthermore, the complexity and interwoven nature of the form helps represent the complex interweaving of perspectives on freedom.

The Ohio Underground Railroad Whistle-Stop Poetry Tour culminated in a Capstone Celebration in Columbus, Ohio's capital. At the Capstone Celebration, we gifted the "How We See Free" broadside to attendees and concluded the event with a four-part reading of the poem. It is our hope that the multitude of voices represented in the poem will resonate with varied audiences and that their unified call for justice and fairness will reverberate far and wide.

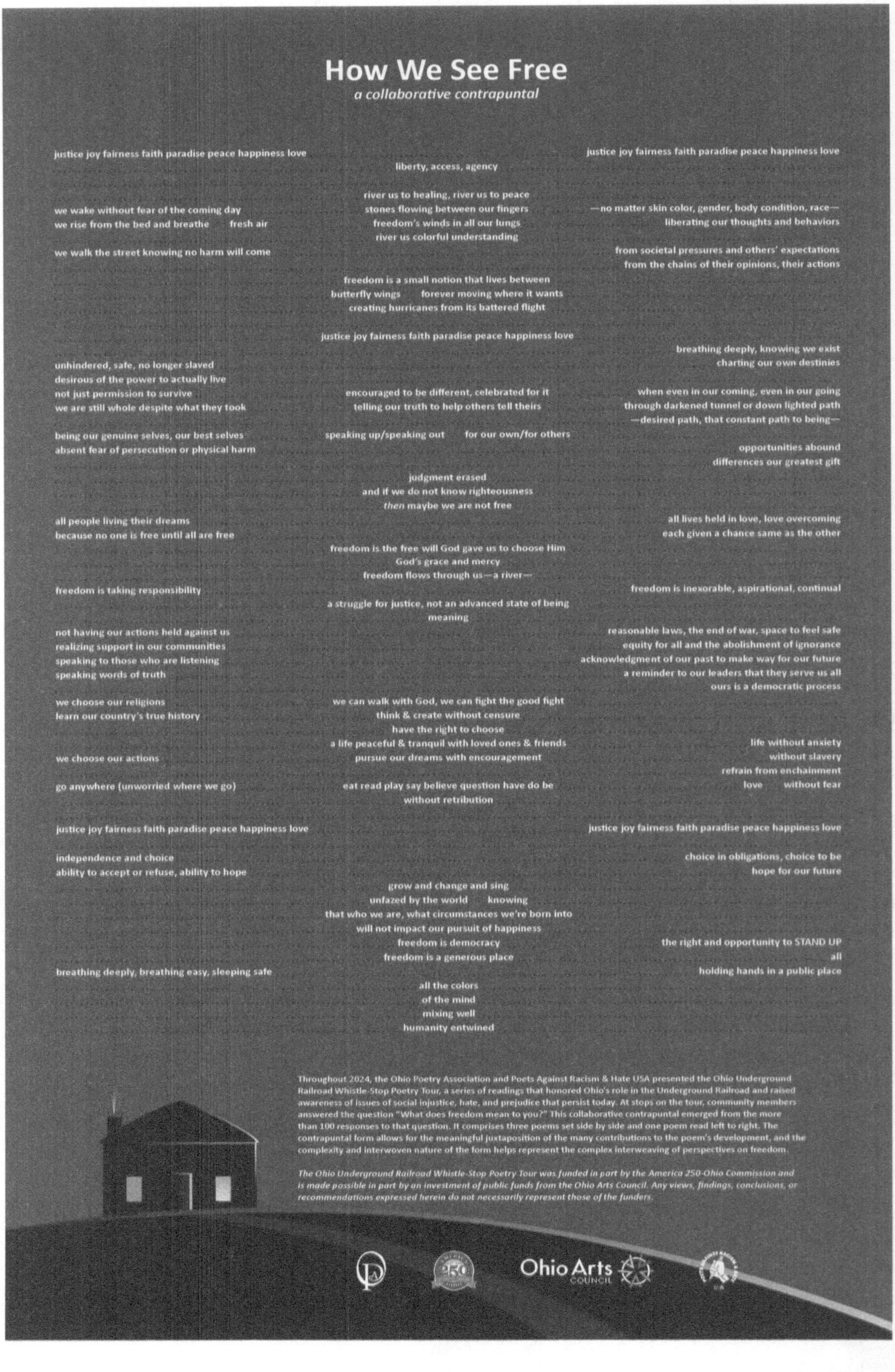

How We See Free
a collaborative contrapuntal

Left column | Middle column | Right column

Left:

justice joy fairness faith paradise peace happiness love

we wake without fear of the coming day
we rise from the bed and breathe   fresh air
we walk the street knowing no harm will come

unhindered, safe, no longer slaved
desirous of the power to actually live
not just permission to survive
we are still whole despite what they took

being our genuine selves, our best selves
absent fear of persecution or physical harm

all people living their dreams
because no one is free until all are free

freedom is taking responsibility

not having our actions held against us
realizing support in our communities
speaking to those who are listening
speaking words of truth

we choose our religions
learn our country's true history

we choose our actions

go anywhere (unworried where we go)

justice joy fairness faith paradise peace happiness love

independence and choice
ability to accept or refuse, ability to hope

breathing deeply, breathing easy, sleeping safe

Middle:

liberty, access, agency

river us to healing, river us to peace
stones flowing between our fingers
freedom's winds in all our lungs
river us colorful understanding

freedom is a small notion that lives between
butterfly wings   forever moving where it wants
creating hurricanes from its battered flight

justice joy fairness faith paradise peace happiness love

encouraged to be different, celebrated for it
telling our truth to help others tell theirs

speaking up/speaking out   for our own/for others

judgment erased
and if we do not know righteousness
then maybe we are not free

freedom is the free will God gave us to choose Him
God's grace and mercy
freedom flows through us—a river—
a struggle for justice, not an advanced state of being
meaning

we can walk with God, we can fight the good fight
think & create without censure
have the right to choose
a life peaceful & tranquil with loved ones & friends
pursue our dreams with encouragement
eat read play say believe question have do be
without retribution

grow and change and sing
unfazed by the world   knowing
that who we are, what circumstances we're born into
will not impact our pursuit of happiness
freedom is democracy
freedom is a generous place

all the colors
of the mind
mixing well
humanity entwined

Right:

justice joy fairness faith paradise peace happiness love

—no matter skin color, gender, body condition, race—
liberating our thoughts and behaviors

from societal pressures and others' expectations
from the chains of their opinions, their actions

breathing deeply, knowing we exist
charting our own destinies

when even in our coming, even in our going
through darkened tunnel or down lighted path
—desired path, that constant path to being—

opportunities abound
differences our greatest gift

all lives held in love, love overcoming
each given a chance same as the other

freedom is inexorable, aspirational, continual

reasonable laws, the end of war, space to feel safe
equity for all and the abolishment of ignorance
acknowledgment of our past to make way for our future
a reminder to our leaders that they serve us all
ours is a democratic process

life without anxiety
without slavery
refrain from enchainment
love   without fear

justice joy fairness faith paradise peace happiness love

choice in obligations, choice to be
hope for our future

the right and opportunity to STAND UP
all
holding hands in a public place

Throughout 2024, the Ohio Poetry Association and Poets Against Racism & Hate USA presented the Ohio Underground Railroad Whistle-Stop Poetry Tour, a series of readings that honored Ohio's role in the Underground Railroad and raised awareness of issues of social injustice, hate, and prejudice that persist today. At stops on the tour, community members answered the question "What does freedom mean to you?" This collaborative contrapuntal emerged from the more than 100 responses to that question. It comprises three poems set side by side and one poem read left to right. The contrapuntal form allows for the meaningful juxtaposition of the many contributions to the poem's development, and the complexity and interwoven nature of the form helps represent the complex interweaving of perspectives on freedom.

The Ohio Underground Railroad Whistle-Stop Poetry Tour was funded in part by the America 250-Ohio Commission and is made possible in part by an investment of public funds from the Ohio Arts Council. Any views, findings, conclusions, or recommendations expressed herein do not necessarily represent those of the funders.

How We See Free

[1]

justice joy fairness faith paradise peace happiness love

we wake without fear of the coming day
we rise from the bed and breathe   fresh air

we walk the street knowing no harm will come
unhindered, safe, no longer slaved
desirous of the power to actually live
not just permission to survive
we are still whole despite what they took

being our genuine selves, our best selves
absent fear of persecution or physical harm

all people living their dreams
because no one is free until all are free

freedom is taking responsibility
not having our actions held against us
realizing support in our communities
speaking to those who are listening
speaking words of truth

we choose our religions
learn our country's true history
we choose our actions
go anywhere (unworried where we go)

justice joy fairness faith paradise peace happiness love

independence and choice
ability to accept or refuse, ability to hope

breathing deeply, breathing easy, sleeping safe

[2]

liberty, access, agency

river us to healing, river us to peace

stones flowing between our fingers
freedom's winds in all our lungs
river us colorful understanding

freedom is a small notion that lives between
butterfly wings   forever moving where it wants
creating hurricanes from its battered flight

justice joy fairness faith paradise peace happiness love

encouraged to be different, celebrated for it
telling our truth to help others tell theirs
speaking up/speaking out   for our own/for others

judgment erased

and if we do not know righteousness
then maybe we are not free

freedom is the free will God gave us to choose Him
God's grace and mercy

freedom flows through us—a river—
a struggle for justice, not an advanced state of being

meaning

we can walk with God, we can fight the good fight
think & create without censure
have the right to choose
a life peaceful & tranquil with loved ones & friends
pursue our dreams with encouragement

eat read play say believe question have do be
without retribution

grow and change and sing
unfazed by the world   knowing
that who we are, what circumstances we're born into
will not impact our pursuit of happiness

freedom is democracy
freedom is a generous place

all the colors
of the mind
mixing well
humanity entwined

[3]

justice joy fairness faith paradise peace happiness love

—no matter skin color, gender, body condition, race—
liberating our thoughts and behaviors
from societal pressures and others' expectations
from the chains of their opinions, their actions

breathing deeply, knowing we exist
charting our own destinies

when even in our coming, even in our going
through darkened tunnel or down lighted path
—desired path, that constant path to being—
opportunities abound
differences our greatest gift

all lives held in love, love overcoming
each given a chance same as the other

freedom is inexorable, aspirational, continual
reasonable laws, the end of war, space to feel safe
equity for all and the abolishment of ignorance
acknowledgment of our past to make way for our future
a reminder to our leaders that they serve us all
ours is a democratic process

life without anxiety
without slavery
refrain from enchainment
love   without fear

justice joy fairness faith paradise peace happiness love

choice in obligations, choice to be
hope for our future

the right and opportunity to STAND UP
all
holding hands in a public place

[4]

justice joy fairness faith paradise peace happiness love
justice joy fairness faith paradise peace happiness love

liberty, access, agency

river us to healing, river us to peace
we wake without fear of the coming day
stones flowing between our fingers
—no matter skin color, gender, body condition, race—
we rise from the bed and breathe   fresh air
freedom's winds in all our lungs
liberating our thoughts and behaviors
river us colorful understanding

we walk the street knowing no harm will come
from societal pressures and others' expectations
from the chains of their opinions, their actions

freedom is a small notion that lives between
butterfly wings   forever moving where it wants
creating hurricanes from its battered flight

justice joy fairness faith paradise peace happiness love

breathing deeply, knowing we exist
unhindered, safe, no longer slaved
charting our own destinies
desirous of the power to actually live
not just permission to survive
encouraged to be different, celebrated for it

when even in our coming, even in our going
we are still whole despite what they took
telling our truth to help others tell theirs
through darkened tunnel or down lighted path
—desired path, that constant path to being—

being our genuine selves, our best selves
speaking up/speaking out   for our own/for others
absent fear of persecution or physical harm

opportunities abound
differences our greatest gift
judgment erased
and if we do not know righteousness
then maybe we are not free

all people living their dreams
all lives held in love, love overcoming
because no one is free until all are free
each given a chance same as the other

freedom is the free will God gave us to choose Him
God's grace and mercy
freedom flows through us—a river—
freedom is taking responsibility
freedom is inexorable, aspirational, continual
a struggle for justice, not an advanced state of being

meaning

not having our actions held against us
reasonable laws, the end of war, space to feel safe
realizing support in our communities
equity for all and the abolishment of ignorance
speaking to those who are listening
acknowledgment of our past to make way for our future
speaking words of truth
a reminder to our leaders that they serve us all
ours is a democratic process

we choose our religions
we can walk with God, we can fight the good fight
learn our country's true history
think & create without censure
have the right to choose
a life peaceful & tranquil with loved ones & friends
life without anxiety

we choose our actions
pursue our dreams with encouragement
without slavery
refrain from enchainment
go anywhere (unworried where we go)
eat read play say believe question have do be
love   without fear
without retribution

justice joy fairness faith paradise peace happiness love
justice joy fairness faith paradise peace happiness love

independence and choice
choice in obligations, choice to be
ability to accept or refuse, ability to hope
hope for our future
grow and change and sing
unfazed by the world   knowing
that who we are, what circumstances we're born into
will not impact our pursuit of happiness

freedom is democracy
the right and opportunity to STAND UP
freedom is a generous place
all
breathing deeply, breathing easy, sleeping safe
holding hands in a public place

all the colors
of the mind
mixing well
humanity entwined

Author Bios

Debbie Allen is a cofounder of Poets Against Racism & Hate USA. A Pushcart Prize nominee, she has performed internationally, and her poetry has appeared in various journals and collections. She has served as an associate poetry editor for *Poets Reading the News*, a committee chair for the Ohio Poetry Association, and a board member for The Watershed Journal Literary Group. Debbie is committed to combating systemic inequities, with much of her poetry tending toward response to injustices. She practices her craft on land originally inhabited by Myaamiaki and Bodéwadmik.

Dr. Susann Moeller, vice-president of the Ohio Poetry Association and vice-chancellor of the National Federation of State Poetry Societies, is an award-winning bilingual poet and editor of the eco-poetry anthologies *Open Earth I, II,* and *III*. She loves to write in the "plotting shed" of her garden turned urban wildlife sanctuary, dances in random places, and believes in the inseparable nature of art and the environment. She promotes poetry as a vehicle for social justice activism and as a genre that enriches every type of experience and vice versa.

Chuck Salmons has received an Ohio Arts Council Individual Excellence Award for poetry and served as a leader for the Ohio Poetry Association. His poems have appeared in numerous journals and anthologies, including *Chiron Review, Pudding Magazine, The Fib Review, Evening Street Review, The Ekphrastic Review, Main Street Rag,* and *I Thought I Heard a Cardinal Sing: Ohio's Appalachian Voices*. He has published three poetry collections: *Stargazer Suite* (11th Hour Press), *Patch Job* (NightBallet Press), and *The Grace of Gazing Inward: Poems in Response to the Art of Alice Carpenter* (Dos Madres Press). Chuck performs with the poetry trio Concrete Wink.

Rikki Santer's poetry has been published widely, and she has received many honors, including several Pushcart and Ohioana book award nominations and a fellowship from the National Endowment for the Humanities. In 2023, Rikki was named Ohio Poet of the Year. She is a member of the teaching artist roster of the Ohio Arts Council and a past vice-president of the Ohio Poetry Association. Her collection *Resurrection Letter* was grand prize short-listed for the Eric Hoffer Book Award, and her forthcoming collection, *Shepherd's Hour*, won the Paul Nemser Book Prize from Lily Poetry Review Books.

Karen Scott is a poet living in Columbus, Ohio. She is a member/supporter of the Ohio Poetry Association and Poets Against Racism & Hate USA, a past participant in the Women of Appalachia Project, and a proud member of the SALON writing group. Her work has been published in several anthologies and reviews, an online "zine," and an online publication and as a broadside. Karen has been a featured poet at several readings and regularly participates in reading at open mics—in person and online.

The Peach Tree

Calley Marotta

Reflection

This piece is a modified excerpt of my book-in-progress, *Blame the Mother: A Memoir*, about my experience mothering a young child through attachment strain. Part One tells the story of my family's move for my first academic job—a move that took us to a foreign place and culture during the height of the COVID 19 pandemic—where we found unlikely community thanks to giving neighbors and a fruit tree. While the entire book is a thought exercise around blame, sections like Part Two use speculative nonfiction to reimagine a world beyond individual blame—a world in which community care thrives. This work has been deeply influenced by traditions of Black Feminism and womanism and Disability Justice. These are movements that encourage writers not to settle for the world that is but dream the world that might be. These authors, activists, and spell-casters include but are not limited to Carmen Maria Machado, Alexis Pauline Gumbs, Octavia Butler, Audre Lorde, Mia Mingus, and Leah Lakshmi Piepzna-Samarasinha.

I am an emerging creative writer who has used art to understand and move through pain. My writing is made possible by the support of my husband and daughter, my daughter's child-care providers and teachers, as well as mentors, colleagues, and friends who encourage and read my writing. Special thanks to the brilliant scientist and author, Debbie Mitchell who first read and liked the Peach Tree section when I worried it might be too wild. I am also grateful to spaces for writers including Heart-Head-Hands, where I found myself writing poetry instead of papers; Lighthouse Writers, where I first dabbled in speculative nonfiction with teachers Sarah Elizabeth Schantz and Harrison Fletcher; and the Write-In-Place groups at the University of Denver. Thank you to the original stewards and caretakers of the land where the peach tree resides and the land upon which I currently live and work—those and their ancestors who have lived amidst violence and broken promises and have yet to receive justice: the Núu-agha-tʉvʉ-pʉ (Ute), Goshute, Nuwuvi (Southern Paiute), Eastern Shoshone, Tsitsista (Cheyenne), and Hinonoeino (Arapaho) Nations. And of course, thank you neighbors, who make daily life a little easier and a little better. You and the peach tree have kept us from feeling alone.

The Peach Tree

Part One

When I chose to be an academic, I chose to move. I agreed to go where I was wanted. I was lucky to be wanted, we all knew. But now it was not just me who would be moving. I would be carrying my husband and child in tow. Children are resilient, people said, when I received a job offer. As we packed up our lives, Andrew never said a word to complain. This was not the first time he had moved for me, and I was not sure if that made it better or worse. Cora was sad to leave the things she knew: her friends, her daycare, her home. I worried it was too much to ask of her to leave these things behind. For me. But things were already decided. We boarded our plane and landed in a city made of churches. I told myself we would begin again.

Before we moved, I worried I would bring my family to a ghost house. In terror, I imagined carrying our boxes and our two-year-old only to find a hole where the house was meant to be. So, to ease our anxiety, our dear friends went to make sure the rental house existed. They were the only people we knew in the city, and they were set to move the next day. But they still graciously toured us around the home by video. In a grainy recording, they scanned across cabinets and rooms before peeking into the yard through a window with crossed wood. "Oh, and there's a peach tree," they said casually. As adults, we had never lived in a whole house. A fruit tree felt baffling. When anyone asked about the move, I responded simply, "There is a peach tree."

The peach tree was large enough for our daughter to sit under and seek respite from the heat. In this place, the shade was dry and cool. I heard the house's owner had a green thumb and had brought the peach tree back to life. It had yet to bloom. That fall, we watched the fuzzy balls turn orange—first a crescent and then a full moon. When I thought of it, I went to check on the peach tree in the garden. I dropped extra pots of water at its feet. I reached up with my palm to pat its trunk and leaves. I used my fingers to pull the vines back as they jumped and coiled around its branches. I pushed them back against the fence, a mother's redirection, to keep the peach tree safe.

The tree exploded with fruit the week we lost power. A windstorm scattered the peaches along the dirt below. I stayed in the dark house without power because there was a pandemic and because we thought the power would return. On the third day, I drove to a parking lot to get service and notify students class was canceled online. For an activity, I let Cora spill a tub of oatmeal on the kitchen floor. She wore her favorite dress with a flouncy skirt and a muted rainbow of birds. She looked up smiling from behind her pixie cut with a handful of sliced peaches the color of her dress when it got damp. But Cora screamed at night when the sun went down and, with it, any existing light.

As the branches of the peach tree dipped with weight, I picked peaches and passed them out to neighbors without touching. Holding plastic bags instead of flesh, I gave them to the men next door who kept to themselves but loved Cora. She sat on the driveway and watched them do ambitious yard projects to a Disco beat. Cora offered them popsicles, and the men took them with both hands. I passed peaches to the girl next door who was Cora's age, an early friend whose mother saved Cora from being lonely when she was home sick, and we still had to work. I gave them to the woman down the street with long gray hair and a one syllable name. She had a geriatric dog named after a flower and a beautiful garden where Cora would stop to pick sparkly rocks. I gave peaches to the post-college grads who lived in a house across the street owned by somebody's mother. The young people seemed to double by the day as they hoisted bags and skis on their car roofs. I dropped peaches at the door of a couple who was dragged down the street by their wild puppy. I offered these fruits, which we had no part in making but received and passed along still. I was too tired to grow anything but Cora.

And, on Cora's late spring birthday, the peach tree was blooming again. Cora's third and fourth birthdays, we celebrated with these neighbors on the porch. We offered a seat and popsicles. They offered gifts. A butterfly kit from the men next door, a suitcase full of art supplies from the couple with the dog, an antique microscope, a box of tiny treasures once used by a kind daughter away at school, a card with stickers signed by the gray-haired woman's dog. As we wrapped our arms around these packages, I tried to tell Cora how lucky we were—that it was unusual to have community this way. I was always trying to explain things she was too young to understand. And still, I thought it needed to be said. This was not something to take for granted.

But things at work, in this new city, had just gotten too hard. I worried I couldn't challenge the writing culture of this place. I was simply anxious and too tired. Our best friends across the street were also leaving to retire on a farm. Somehow, that made it feel like the right time to leave. One day, when we were having a driveway picnic, this friend appeared in a collared shirt. It was a surprise—he worked on a nearby farm, and we had never seen him in anything but t-shirts and jeans. But now he was placing a dish towel over his arm and presenting a flower in a vase with a bottle of sparkling water. He was showing us the label and pouring sparkly bubbles into a glass. With peach juice on our palms, we were still giggling as he crossed the street to go home. When we decided to leave the block that had become our home, the owners told us it was a good time. They were planning to sell. As I listened to this news on the phone, I was grateful we were not being uprooted against our will. But all I really heard was that they were going to sell the peach tree.

Part Two

When you think of it, you go to check on me in the garden. You drop extra pots of water at my feet. You reach up with your palm to pat my trunk and leaves. You and your daughter do this together, until, one day, with your hands on my spine, you notice a vine growing along the fence. The vine jumps and coils itself around my branch. You cannot believe the vine is so alive—that it can jump and cling. You use your fingers to untangle the leaves and push the vine away from me. Like a good mother, you are protective. You tell it to keep its hands to itself.

But each day, the vine creeps further toward and then up and around me. Some days you take kitchen shears and slice the rope back. Other times you rip it with your hands, putting force on the center until it cracks into pieces. But then you become busy, distracted, sad. You take your eyes from me. Weeks pass. You are not sleeping. And in your daze, you miss the signs. Unencumbered, the vine slides along the pavement path and the cracked cement until it reaches the threshold of the house. With a rustle, it comes up through the window with the crossed wood and seeps between the panes. There you lay in your daughter's room. The vine begins to slide through the shag carpeting. That thick shag swallows the vine as the carpet swallowed your fingers and toes. Your eyes close for a moment. Cora's limbs finally calm. You do not know the vine has swallowed me. You do not know it is coming for Cora when it finds you there on the floor.

You first feel the pressure on your knees, then a cord along your torso. It rocks you, holding you tight while you allow your eyes to rest. Just for a moment, the vine meets your hunger for comfort. It holds you the way you long to be held. But the vine is not satisfied. It wants more than you can give. Your lungs strain, but you know it is useless to struggle. So, you stop pushing. You let your muscles go soft and limp, leaving space between your torso and the vine's folds. Like a cat takes her umbilical cord, you put the vine in your mouth and cut it with your teeth. Then you twirl your body out of the rest of the cord. You are dancing. You move across the carpet and pull the vine like a garden hose back to the yard. I gaze upon it around your shoulder, and it seems suddenly thin and small—even weak. I realize it no longer scares me. You do not curse the vine and simply pat it lightly. You know it is just trying to survive.

The next day, you rise from the shag carpet at dawn. And in your lemon robe, you go to knock on neighbors' doors. They wake, rumpled and sleepy, to gather in the garden. Together without words, you open the shed and rummage through unfamiliar tools. Someone knows what they are and how to help; and so, you make a plan. You remove old fencing made of wood and wire. It is a structure, a sculpture, a collage. You place it upon the earth at a distance from the peach tree. Then you take the vine in your hands and, with your daughter and husband and neighbors, you weave and wrap it round and round. Now the vine can hold and climb without my branches. I am relieved at my new-found safety, as I watch you, together, offer the redirection of a mother's hand.

Over the next few weeks, you watch my fruit ripen fully on my limbs. Balls of fruit fall to the ground. The dark orange color seeps out of the garden and into the neighbors' yards. I smell like the color—sour and deep. Squirrels and birds nibble my flesh. You tell yourself it is only natural—that I am doing as I was designed. But the changing season still makes you feel melancholy. The lines along your mouth soften as you watch the decomposing fruit. I am transforming—pointing forward and back in time. You begin to imagine a future for my parts. In your mind's eye, you see the hard pits carried off to root elsewhere. Beneath the ground, you imagine the parts, my offspring, sleeping until they are ready to break the surface again.

Author Bio

Calley Marotta is a writer, mother, teacher, and friend. She teaches writing at the University of Denver where her work focuses on the relationship between literacy, justice, and carework. You can find her creative nonfiction in *The Journal of Multimodal Rhetorics, Atticus Review, The Los Angeles Review, The Maine Review,* and *MUTHA Magazine*. She thanks family, colleagues, writing groups, and students for supporting and inspiring her writing.

Book Reviews

From the Book and New Media Review Editor's Desk

Jessica Shumake, Editor
University of Notre Dame

My family and I recently drove from the Midwest to Tucson just before monsoon season to appreciate the smell of creosote and our community there. A poem by Ana Moffet and mosaic tile art installation by Nina Borgia-Aberle titled *Gratitude* greets all-comers immediately outside of the free, fully shaded, disability accessible, public recreation pool we frequented during our visit: "I thank the Earth for feeding my body. I thank the sun for warming my bones. I thank the trees for the air that I breathe. An' I thank the water for nourishing my soul." The gift of an open and accessible public swimming pool reminded me that enjoying the offerings in my immediate surroundings can nourish my physical and mental well-being.

Playful attention, laughter, and joy animate the reviews in this issue. Jennifer W. Grauvogl's review of *Community Listening: Stories, Hauntings, Possibilities* demonstrates that listening is not passive, but as an active commitment to living with others, attending to absences, and stepping into discomfort. Eileen Lagman and Elizabeth Keylon's *Reading, Writing, and Queer Survival* similarly reminds us that literacy is never just written, oral, and multimodal communication but rather one's sense of self is affected and mediated through the places, humans and non-humans, and materialities that are part of a whole ecology. All three reviewers featured in this issue ask us to expand our notions of what counts as meaning-making, and who and what get to matter.

I am grateful to the reviewers whose writing challenges *CLJ* readers to listen harder, laugh louder, and speak and write more candidly. I also extend my deep thanks to Isabel Baca and Libby Catchings, who are the editors of this issue and who were generous in their timeline to see these two excellent reviews through to publication. Everyone's contributions remind me that our ability to hear and be heard is a gift and an ethical responsibility that can enliven the communities we love and serve, to approach each day with openness and a renewed sense of imagination.

Community Listening: Stories, Hauntings, Possibilities

Edited by Jenn Fishman, Romeo García, and Lauren Rosenberg
Perspectives on Writing, The WAC Clearinghouse, 2025, pp. 255

Reviewed by Jennifer W. Grauvogl
Eastern New Mexico University

We are our stories. We harvest our personal narratives from our cultural histories. We plant our futures in the soil of the micro, macro, and meso narratives we hear shouted and whispered about our situational limits and potentials. In Jenn Fishman, Romeo García, and Lauren Rosenberg's *Community Listening: Stories, Hauntings, Possibilities*, the editors and authors acknowledge the transformational power of equitable collective listening, or community listening, in human meaning/story making.

A definition of community listening that includes every facet explored by the contributors in this collection does not yet exist because the editors listened carefully to their authors' ideas and granted wide rhetorical spaces to explore how deep listening can create comprehensive transformation. This collection of ten chapters range from scholarship centering academic listening of Aryan Nations' texts to experiments in community listening to create bipartisan agreements; however, the unifying imbrication appears in the way authors entangle ways of "knowing individually and collectively, past and recent, and how those ways weave together and change through the listening practices" all to explore "what listening means and how it can be used and understood, now and in the future" (23).

While each chapter uses different lenses, different definitions and/or terms, and different results of community listening, each contributor agrees that community listening—in all its varieties—inevitably produces two more questions for every one answer unearthed. They also agree that open ears pry open the hearts and minds of the listeners and the people being truly heard. Each chapter concludes that listening is only a starting point; actions (or inactions) must follow, but those actions center on acknowledging that listening weaves together independence with dependence and interdependence.

The book is written for anyone who seeks meaning, not necessarily "disciplines of the university," but for anyone who has ears and wants to hear others to create relationships built on an ethos of care that includes curiosity, concern, and responsibility (4). Community organizers, activists, politicians, advocates for vulnerable populations, and any student of humanity will benefit from approaches using collective listening as a form of deeper understanding. This collection can gently push (or shove) readers out of their complacency to ponder what it could mean to listen with, to, through, and as a community, then think/dream/act collectively with humane compassion.

Although written for anyone seeking a greater connection as a collective of humanity, the editors' preface is an academic survey of the literature that situates the collection as an organic result of decades of listening research. The introduction prepares the readers to listen carefully to scholars whose qualitative research might easily be dismissed and defunded in today's climate of screaming and smothering to erase conflicting stories. However, the depth of our humanity derives from the layers of our stories; the more voices the collective hears, the greater our capacity to create humanity-centered communities.

While academic listening studies have been around for decades, Fishman, García, and Rosenberg's review starts with a special issue of *Community Literacy Journal* inspired by the 2017 Conference on Community Writing and is "the first concerted effort to collect academic accounts of community listening" (5). Rather than solving all the mysteries found in the space of collective listening theory, the collection widens the abyss. The editors' introduction situates their collection in that abyss of the unknown. The collection offers an array of experiences and practices that could inspire readers to open their ears to the communities around and within them. To prepare their readers for the trip, the editors provide an array of definitions of listening, situate listening as an academic practice on par with reading, writing, and speaking, then flashback to listening studies that have planted seeds harvested from even earlier works.

To illustrate how so many ideas can be separate but can still create beauty, the editors use a metaphor of a starry night sky. They imagine each historical and current researcher as a star. Each star has its own light, width, gravity, and orbit, just like each contributor has their own take on what collective listening in their work looks like, means, and does. The introduction puts several rhetorical rock stars into constellations that shine light on the collection's authors. Each has their own scholarship, approach, and focus, but they all form pictures that create the constellation of listening studies. Krista Ratcliffe's work in rhetorical listening and eavesdropping shines light on Jacqueline Jones Royster's studies, which center on finding and listening to smothered voices. The editors contrast Ratcliffe and Royster with Linda Flower's work, which may not seem to center rhetorical listening, but is intensely collaborative, which tacitly requires intense listening. When the readers listen carefully to the texts of the stars in these academic constellations, they will see that the narrative that emerges is one that tells us there are more voices in human history than there are stars. Still, we are all needed to complete the sky.

The editors separate the collection into three parts. In Part 1: Hauntings and Possibilities, contributors explore how listening to "the absent presence of the past in the present" (13) can strip macro narratives back to reveal buried micro stories about victimized and villainized humans. Part 2: Stories of Sustaining Community introduces listening to community text—like art, music, and letters—as a synesthetic way to experience a listening that involves the ears, eyes, and heart, but touches to the bones., Part 3: Negotiating Self and Community, moves from listening as a passive or quasi-passive activity into a realm where listening is a form of action that validates the speaker's human experience.

In Part 1, authors listen to incarcerated people, read to hear differently abled voices, and struggle with a narrative about the ethics of excluding any voices in honest histories of racism. Their methods differ, but the authors' conclusions establish listening as a foundation for true inclusion.

Chapter 1, Sally F. Benson's "Getting Closer to Mass Incarceration: Proximate Listening as Community Activism," employs *proximate listening* as a practice for community listening that focuses on identifying how we listen, how we let others' stories unshape us, and how we report our listening. The haunting is the histories that adumbrate ugly societal truths that our eyes slide off of in privileged embarrassment. Benson's *proximate listening* in a prison community challenged her ideas of what listening means. Benson challenges readers to "dwell near enough, long enough, silent enough" not just to notice "our relational differences," but also "acknowledge our misunderstandings, and empty ourselves to make room for new ways of understanding" (43). Proximate listening asks listeners to pause their judgment and even their philanthropy and just hear—hear the hunger for validation, not solutions—a hearing that begins and ends with love.

In Chapter 2, "Crafting Crip Space Through Disabled Political Advocacy: #CriptTheVote as Community Listening," Ada Hubrig asks how disability advocacy is shaped by community listening, searches for a definition of other-abled community listening, and queries if disabled advocacies merely reaffirm disabilities as inherent flaws. Hubrig argues that disability activism means creating spaces for communities to hear the stories of differently abled people as they "push back against the dismissal of disabled activist methods" (59). Again, readers are faced with ghosts of assumptions that haunt the fringes of our narratives; these ghosts will terrify listeners less as #CriptTheVote gives them shape and substance in the ears of the community listeners with the hearts to truly hear.

Chapter 3 "Keeping Bad Company: Listening to Aryan Nations in the Archives" by Patty Wilde, Mitzi Ceballos, and Wyn Andrews Richards flips the script as a group of students who are haunted by the voices of vile racists attempt to negotiate the context in which offensive archival information and documents are circulated by the university to students and the local community. Their attempts taught the authors that listening in silence can be as effective—or as symbolic—as advocating for change. The haunting forced the authors to reconsider their own biases and abilities to listen to all voices, even those objectionable to their own experiences. While these scholars felt their venture failed, they are determined to vigilantly continue their work to build a community where productive conversations are possible.

Part 2: Stories of Sustaining Community centers listening to stories that "showcase community experiences" like public art, radio programs, and letters to and from incarcerated people (18). The contributors in Part 2 expand the definition of listening and thus illustrate the "multiplicity of listening relationships" (19). Listening becomes more than hearing; listening becomes a way of creating a space where people can see, feel, and hear stories in ways that create and reveal humanity in community.

In Chapter 4, "The Public Art of Listening: Relational Accountability and The Painted Desert Project," Kyle Boggs takes the reader for a listening tour through the Navajo Nation via public art as the voice of the community. Boggs asks readers to listen to art whose living intent is to "serve as advocacy and community writing," which then spotlights—and in some cases floodlights—community experience (94). Looking becomes a form of listening when the eyes take in the images without judgment, without supplanting their own stories, and with trust that creates a relationship between the community, the artist, and the seeing-listener. That relationship has the power to ignite "critical reflections about how we are constituted by colonial structures" and can result in "public engagement that invites stronger, more empathetic alliances across differences" (113) and thus sustain even imperiled communities.

Karen R. Tellez-Trujillo's community-sustaining story, Chapter 5: "The DJ as Relational Listener and Creator of an Ethos of Community Listening," explores relational listening as a form of community listening. Radio is a medium that weaves together listeners through the power of music. Music is the voice of the community; we listen with our bodies, hearts, as well as ears. Music creates community as people listen to the songs that become their own personal soundtracks, and as they hear in another's voice the same longing that's tucked in their souls. As Tellez-Trujillo reflects on the southwest Sunday afternoon oldies program and its deliberately relationally listening DJ, she posits that it is through listener participation that "the listener builds upon memories carried form the past, associated with music by layering new memories" and that music becomes a site of community/relational listening (130).

Prison's most cruel form of punishment is the isolation that prisoners experience from their home communities. The incarcerated communities do not often sustain their members' well-being. Prison literacy educators and researchers, Alexandra J. Cavallaro, Wendy Hinshaw, and Tobi Jacobi craft Chapter 6, "Listening In: Letter Writing and Rhetorical Resistance Behind Bars," as a reflection on how *community-centered listening* in prisons validates the humanity of inmates. The authors of this chapter ask readers to peer in at a community and consider how that looking equates to listening. They also ask readers to step outside of their complacency and enter spaces that challenge their listening resilience by reaching out to communities who are isolated, marginalized, and demonized with a humble request to share their experiences, their stories, and their hearts.

The last section, Part 3: Negotiating Self and Community, pushes readers towards intersections of community and self that are created through community listening. In these chapters, readers (1) hear how deep listening to stories creates community (2) even when (if not especially) those stories challenge the listener to sit with uncomfortable topics. The last chapter, "Daunting Community Listening: Designing and Implementing a Community Listening Framework and Accountability Group for Undergraduate Students," is strategically situated as the final chapter because it builds on and synthesizes the ideas from the previous nine chapters to underscore how listening deeply is required to enter communities. Deep listening can strip us of our false and under-informed stories, and, if we let it, the discomfort of relearning can propel listeners to meaningful action.

Individuals' stories create community in Bailey M. Oliver-Blackburn, April Chatham-Carpenter, and Carol L. Thompson's Chapter 7: "Civic Community Listening: The Nexus of Storytelling and Listening Within Civic Communities." Only a person with their head buried deeply in the sand could be unaware of the divisive political climate the 21st century has gifted the human world. But the National Braver Angels have banded together to create local spaces for citizens to share their stories—and spaces to hear each other's stories in a practice of social community listening, which results in increased perspective taking and decreased vitriol; storytelling and listening become an invitation to be civically engaged in civility. The more participants in National Braver Angels' forums engage in *civic community listening*, by intentionally listening to each other's stories, the more people want to participate. The more people who participate, the more voices, stories, and perspectives are heard—and the more people start to understand each other.

In Chapter 8, Mary P. Sheridan, Cate Fosl, Kelly Kinahan, Carrie Mott, Angela Storey, and Shelley Thomas' "Community Listening In, With, and Against Whiteness at a PWI" frames a conversation about a university that has not fully addressed structural racism. All the authors are white women. They elected to implement methodologies of listening silently to the stories that uncovered "who is privileged and who is muted" (177). The women found that their work raised more questions than they answered. They found themselves pondering how white women can "foster spaces that destabilize whiteness while we call in and remain open to being called out?" (193). How can people with privilege listen to people to educate other people of privilege without co-opting others' stories? These authors raised hard questions and faced difficult situations, but have resolved to keep questioning, keep challenging themselves, and keep listening.

Building on the self-examinations and honest reflection of the previous chapter, Chapter 9, "On Being in It," by Katie W. Powell, is a narrative study of the murder of Dr. James Monroe, an enslaver, killed by his rebelling slaves. The reader listens to Powell's journey into history and her uncovering of the complex and violent history of a geographical region still haunted by unacknowledged stories. Through *storied community listening*—which Powell defines as looking for narratives that have been historically left out and/or covered up—listeners may find that those stories contradict each other. Competing stories do not have to result in increased controversy but could be "methods for employing counterstory" that could move toward reconciliation through an honest appraisal of differences (22).

The collection weaves together the whats and the whys. Then it ends with a powerful how-to in Chapter 10: "Daunting Community Listening: Designing and Implementing a Community Listening Framework and Accountability Group for Undergraduate Students" in which Keri Epps and Rowie Kirby-Straker with Basey Beiswenger, Zoe Chamberlain, Hannah Hill, Lauren Robertson, and Kaitlyn Taylor take on hard community listening and find that pain is not only a great teacher but also the greatest catalyst for internal and external change. The researchers name their methodology: *daunting community listening,* which acknowledges the discomfort and fear that honest listening engenders, especially in the sincerest listener. This final chapter of the collection shares a narrative that centers voices commonly decentered in education and provides a detailed program that the university and community partner utilized to recenter listening as a form of relationship building. The readers of the collection will need to listen hard to this last chapter. Listening may seem like passive inaction, but the internal rearranging that authentic listening initiates will transform the teachable person.

The collection's strength is demonstrating that community listening is a powerful methodology that can inform academic research at a humane level. Because the authors are academics and educators, their texts ask readers to intentionally study, formally teach, and deliberately learn ethical community listening. These asks are made with compassion, and as an academic, I cheer them on. However, the world my students and I live in screams at them, shoves fabricated stories down their throats, and demands they align with one side of a socially constructed binary instead of seeking to understand the multiverse of humanity. The editors and authors have given readers intellectual starting points. As an educator, I am thrilled with the conversations. As a professor, I wonder if I can listen loudly enough to guide my students. As a human silenced by a screaming world, I often wonder if Siri is the only one listening to me.

Reading, Writing, and Queer Survival: Affects, Matterings, and Literacies Across Appalachia

Caleb Pendygraft
UP of Kentucky, 2025, 186 pp.

Reviewed by Eileen Lagman and Elizabeth Keylon
University of Wisconsin-Madison

Caleb Pendygraft opens his prologue to *Reading, Writing, and Queer Survival* with a vignette that features a mountain, a Bible verse, and his grandparents—his grandfather sitting on a worn recliner and his grandmother cooking eggs and bacon on a well-seasoned skillet. His grandfather asks him, "Do you really believe if you prayed hard enough and had faith the grain of a mustard seed, you could move that mountain out there?" The mountain was a hill that his grandfather and father created by carving out Appalachian soil, and the Bible verse was Matthew 17:20. When Pendygraft returned to his grandparents' house in Appalachia years later, after coming out, his grandfather was dead, and the mountain had been excavated.

What is noticeable in this vignette is the limited role literacy as text or writing plays. Pendygraft says that his grandparents could be analyzed in this scene as his "literacy sponsors." Drawing on this established literacy theory, Pendygraft notes that other scholars might look at this scene of literacy and see that his grandparents enabled his religious literacies from a young age. But he argues that relying on this analysis alone would be missing the point: "I find that conventional notions of literacy sponsorship fail to account for all the complexities of meaning-making and power relations in queer lives" (xi). As such, Pendygraft depicts a Biblical literacy that is not as alive in the scene as his grandfather's recliner and dose of insulin medication, or his granny's eggs and bacon sizzling on the cast-iron skillet, or for that matter, the mountain that appeared to have up and left when he returned eight years later.

To understand this scene, and the potential of literacy in this scene, Pendygraft argues for a theory of "animate literacies," drawing on Mel Chen's theory of animacy and biopolitics, where animacy can be described as a "quality of agency, awareness, mobility and liveliness" (Chen 2, qtd. in Pendygraft xi). This includes the material world or nonhuman actors. He writes, "literacy involves an amalgam of the human and nonhuman, organic and inorganic, stretching across a spectrum of concrete materiality to the abstraction of belief" (xi). In other words, making the case for a less human-centric notion of literacy, one that focuses less on human-to-human interactions and more on the underexplored elements that animate us, he writes: "Words typed on a screen, read aloud or written down are not the only markers of literacy" (xi). Ultimately, Pendygraft aims to theorize the nonhuman in literacy through his own qualitative research in the form of ethnographic and autoethnographic storytelling. He does this to understand how queerness, literacy, and Appalachia shape and are shaped by one another, and in doing so, offers an expansion of posthumanist literacy as a theoretical framework.

In doing this work, Pendygraft's book can be connected to scholars of literacy who have questioned the centrality of the human, and even the centrality of "writing" in our research on literacy. This includes posthumanist and new materialist approaches by rhetoricians, compositionists, and educational literacy scholars, many of whom are cited in Pendygraft's book. One might also connect Pendygraft's aim to Catherine Prendergast's notion, after researching literacy in an undergraduate research lab, that Writing to Learn approaches may overemphasize the role of writing in science research, and that literacy scholars might instead think of writing as one voice in a larger chorus of embodied and sensate learning. Similarly, in Evan Watkin's critique of literacy studies, he argues that literacy scholars should be less concerned with documenting new and more literacies and more on the affective and economic conditions in which literacy subjects are constituted.

Finally, we might draw upon Kevin M. Leander and Christian Ehret's question from *Affect in Literacy Learning and Teaching* as one way to frame Pendygraft's work. In their introduction on the role affect might play in our understanding of literacy learning, they ask: "Where did life go?" (7). In posing this question, they hope to "recover, in literacy studies, a sense of the energy, possibility, and feeling of life within the everyday ways that people engage with literacy" (8). Pendygraft's book can be seen as an answer to this question. He demonstrates through this vignette, and throughout his book, that it is not the traditionally conceived literacy—the bible verse—that animates the scene, nor are his literacy sponsors what bring animacy. Instead, it is the mountain that is filled with life. In other words, his answer to the question "where did life go" would be found in the matterings and affects of place.

Indeed, Pendygraft associates literacy with unexpected objects: some that are more obviously connected to text-based literacy, such as tarot cards, knowledge of state-wide water heater regulations, coming out stories, novels, poems, and sexual health advocacy campaigns. But others are less obvious: shorts worn during Pride, a phallic-shaped candle in a tarot reader's trailer closet, scars, drugs, condoms. For Pendygraft, literacy as alphabetic text-based inscription may not be the most important aspect of understanding queer life in Appalachia. Though writing may show up at the scene, it occurs alongside matterings and affects, as well as literacies more broadly conceived, that become part of the networked assemblage of queer experience in Appalachia. In fact, "reading and writing can clash with animate literacies" such that text-based literacy might butt up against the work of "animate literacies," but the "friction it causes still does something in the world" (107).

After a Prologue that lays out the major claims and objectives of the book, Pendygraft's first two chapters lay out his theoretical approach and set up the case studies in Chapters Three and Four. Chapter One "Animacy, Literacy and Queer Agency" includes a brief history of Pendygraft's notion of literacy studies and forwards his main theoretical concept: animate literacies. He grounds this concept on the critique that literacy studies, at least from a Western perspective, have "narrowly focused on the human domain in its treatment of literacy" (xix). Animate literacies, he argues, defines literacy as "energentic exchange rather than only an ability or resource" (4) and includes two elements: literacy matters and literacy affects.

While chronicling literacy approaches—ranging from Royster's notion language as a doing, Gee's definition of literacy bound to being, Brandt's definition of literacy sponsorship, and Alexander's notion of sexual literacy—he amends these theories through posthumanist notions of material agency, where materiality in literacy studies does not refer to only texts and those who create them, but also other objects and matterings. Importantly, Pendygraft draws on queer theory to explain that this shift in perspectives is a kind queering of the scene of literacy: the recentering of literacy toward a "complex web of agential relations" is queer (12)—it can "invert the hierarchies of the inappropriate, the nonhuman, the in order to create new meaning" (13).

After establishing a definition of animate literacies as "an exchange of forces, emanating from a combination of sign systems, performances, and the sensate, which flow between human and nonhuman agents, in and through particular places, in order to effect change, creating new ways of being with and meaning-making" (18), Chapter 2 describes how animate literacies matter in queer Appalachia. As such, Pendygraft both complicates queer and Appalachia through the notion of animacy. Pendygraft, in particular, uses Chen's theory of animacy as a model for disrupting the hierarchy of animacy. Animacy, as defined here, is both a material and affective construct that is shaped by race, sexuality, and other biopolitical factors and, in turn, shapes the world around it, challenging separations or classifications of life and nonlife.

Pendygraft aims, then, to apply this theory of animacies, "to more immediate ways" and to "affective and material conditions of literacy" to "reveal that literacy is, like animacies, nonneutral" (2). Moreover, like Chen, Pendygraft invokes this theory as it intersects with queerness and queer theory relating to nonconventional reproduction, sex, and intimacy as well as just general subversions of normativities (2). In explaining his own use of queer, he says, "I take queering to be disruptive, disorienting, wrought with failures—embracing mess, the profane, and the ugly, all the while knowing that queering can undo selfhood and imagine possibilities not yet actualized" (3). However, he does not shy away from the initial relationship between queerness and nonnormative forms of bodies or sex as an act. The added layers of rhetorical framing, namely the application of new materialist ideas and posthumanist principles, prompt him to offer a new definition of literacy.

An important part of understanding the dynamics on animate literacies in Appalachia specifically is acknowledging that Appalachia is queer. Pendygraft writes, "It is in otherness, strangeness, indeterminacy and resistance that Appalachia and queerness overlap" (28). To attend to animate literacies in Appalachia, he details a method of "metaphoric tracking," which he describes as a queer methodology. As an adaption of Laurie Gries' iconographic tracking, metaphoric tracking centers queer storytelling and searches for metaphors in queer storytelling because of their inherent articulations of relationality (i.e. how one kind of thing can be understood and experienced in terms of another). He notes, "metaphoric tracking looks for metaphors in queer storytelling as indicators of relationality on all levels" (41). Put another way, "Queer metaphors give us insight into the constellations of actants that comprise animate literacies" (xxi).

Chapter Three "Matters of the Closet" focuses on one queer metaphor: coming out of the closet. Using the method of metaphoric tracking, Pendygraft details the coming out narrative of one of his participants, Justin, an Appalachian man from southeastern Ohio, and describes "the human and non-human literacies" or sponsors "that dissuade and enable his coming out" (xxi). In attending to what he calls "literacy matters of the closet," he poses "questions that grapple with the social, systemic, and/or lived realities that accompany coming out, but also contemplate what other *things* matter in coming out" (54). That is, rather than thinking about "coming out" as the literacy practice or rhetorical act, as other rhetoric and composition scholarship has done, Pendygraft identifies the objects and matterings of Justin's closet, the "unaccounted actants" (54) that serve to animate the literacies of coming out. In doing this, he shows that metaphoric tracking for *literacy matters* highlight "metaphors that permit a glimpse into how being with objects and places in literacy is as equally important as the ability to read and write and all other acts of discernment" (55).

While Chapter Three focuses on *literacy matters*, Chapter Four focuses on *literacy affects*, which allows Pendygraft to further explain his definition of literacy as "an exchange of forces" (73). The chapter highlights the stories of four focal participants, all bisexual cisgender women, and moments of queer affinities in their lives where literacy exists as part of energetic exchange, and the affects of literacy that exist long after the literacy encounter. Here, Pendygraft understands that exchange is not a transaction, but is centered on change that comes through some object's agency. As part of this exploration, he argues that literacy affects are "states of being" as opposed to personal emotions and explains that "affinities" are the "formation of affects when they brush up against bodies" (75). The case studies in this chapter range in emotional tone and in the ways that literacy, queerness, and Appalachia appear in the stories. From Lara's campaign to get condoms into her college dorms to stories of drug use and assault (for which Pendygraft offers trigger warnings), these case studies start from traditional notions of literacy but reveal "how affinities with and for others form through literacy practices and can affect us even after reading and writing is over" (xxi).

Chapter Five, "Carrying Mountains to the Sea," is Pendygraft's concluding chapter and his self-identified "praxis" chapter, where he "stor[ies] a pedagogy of animate literacies" (xxi). However, the chapter also appears more like an autoethnographic account of queer Appalachian animate literacies in Pendygraft's life. The chapter is situated at the Massachusetts Maritime Academy, where Pendygraft is a professor, and the Cape Cod Canal, as a place that animates literacy, is central to the pedagogy Pendygraft describes. Pendygraft focuses on his experience teaching his Appalachian Culture undergraduate course, where Appalachia—its mountains, its traditions, its "folkways," and its literacies—are animated through various teaching practices he enacts. To bring Appalachia to Cape Cod, Pendygraft brings agents, human and non-human, that animate Appalachian histories and stories for his students, including the red bandana from which the term "redneck" originates, the banjo, the making of soap, and Appalachian artists including musician Susan Pepper and novelist Carter Sickles. Pendygraft also details how his students animate Appalachia in new ways through their research, prompting Pendygraft to consider how each place—the ocean of Cape Cod and the mountains of Appalachia—animates, for him, a sense of home.

In this concluding chapter, Pendygraft notes that Appalachia animated his own literacy: "Appalachia has funneled the flow of this entire manuscript" (73), taking him in directions he would not have otherwise planned. Therefore, Pendygraft's work follows existing work in Appalachian rhetorics and literacies, but rather than focus solely on class dynamics, poverty, or illiteracy stereotypes, he focuses on the queerness of Appalachia, particularly on the fact, he claims, that there is no one Appalachia. As he acknowledges, part of the difficulty of studying Appalachia is that it does not exist as a singular place. It exists instead in the plural stretching from New England through parts of the Midwest and into the Deep South existing in as a multitudinous place of queer and/or strange contradictions rather than the sort of simplicity that the singular term Appalachia implies.

For this reason, community literacy scholars and literacy researchers more broadly will find that Pendygraft's manuscript offers conceptual vocabulary for thinking about how communities and community literacies are "animated" by human and non-human actors. Importantly, Pendygraft also offers both alignment with and challenges to the notion of community literacy as place-based, whether as bounded spatially or made through literacy exchanges or the circulation of public rhetoric. He notes that "place takes a greater significance with animate literacies, in terms of both where we study literacy and how we theorize its goal in treating place as actively participating in the study" (xix). And importantly, Pendygraft notes, Appalachia is queer and Appalachia has animacy. Because of this, Pendygraft's work might prompt community literacy practitioners and scholars to explore emergent and animated notions of place further.

Community literacy scholars will find resonance in Pendygraft's focus on community knowledge over institutional knowledge, in methods for collecting and analyzing stories, and in his understanding of community as underscored by relationality and affective affinities. In particular, he unpacks the relationship between self and place, "affected and mediated through" literacy practices (95). While some may consider the small sample size as unable to provide generalizable research, Pendygraft could easily counter that this may well be the nature of queer research and research in queer Appalachia. At the same time, Pendygraft's analysis squeezes out insight from each piece of a participant's story, noting animate materiality that might not otherwise be acknowledged as part of reading the world and the self. The work that Pendygraft is doing is trying to carve out an academic space for the messy, painful, scary, and strange realities of literacy, and he smudges the neat lines of traditional literacy scholarship beautifully with dick candles, water heaters, tarot cards, and all the incidentals in between.

Work Cited

Leander, Kevin, and Christian Ehret, eds. *Affect in Literacy Learning and Teaching: Pedagogies, Politics and Coming to Know.* Routledge, 2019.

PARLOR PRESS
EQUIPMENT FOR LIVING

Now with Parlor Press!

Studies in Rhetorics and Feminism
   New Series Editors: Jessica Enoch and Sharon Yam

Critical Conversations in Higher Education Leadership
   Series Editor: Victor E. Taylor

New Releases

Storied Objects: A Graphic Narrative Reflection on Material Metaphors and Digital Writing by Erin Kathleen Bahl

Xeno >> Glossia: An Illuminated Study of Christine de Pizan by Marci Vogel

Rhetorical Reception: One Hundred and Fifty Years of Arguing with Sex in Education by Carolyn Skinner

City Housekeeping: Women's Labor Rhetorics and Spaces for Solidarity, 1886–1911 by Liane Malinowski

Kenneth Burke's Rhetoric of Identification by Tilly Warnock

The Forever Colony by Victor Villanueva

Inclusive Aims: Rhetoric's Role in Reproductive Justice edited by Heather Brook Adams and Nancy Myers

Forthcoming in 2026

Shaping Rhetorical Studies: The Research of RSA Fellows, with Commentary edited by Cheryl Glenn and Richard Leo Enos

Teaching and Learning with Rhetorical Listening: Alternatives to Self-Censorship and Silence in High School and College Classrooms edited by Krista Ratcliffe and Jessica Rivera-Mueller

Check Out Our Website!

Discounts, blog, open access titles, instant downloads, and more.

parlorpress.com

CLJ **Discount:** Use CLJ20 at checkout to receive a 20% discount on all titles not on sale through November 30, 2025.

www.ingramcontent.com/pod-product-compliance
Lightning Source LLC
Chambersburg PA
CBHW021938160426
43195CB00011B/1140